Congressional
Research Service
Informing the legislative debate since 1914 _____

Maritime Territorial and Exclusive Economic Zone (EEZ) Disputes Involving China: Issues for Congress

Ronald O'Rourke
Specialist in Naval Affairs

July 3, 2014

Congressional Research Service

7-5700

www.crs.gov

R42784

Summary

China's actions for asserting and defending its maritime territorial and exclusive economic zone (EEZ) claims in the East China (ECS) and South China Sea (SCS), particularly since late 2013, have heightened concerns among observers that ongoing disputes over these waters and some of the islands within them could lead to a crisis or conflict between China and a neighboring country such as Japan, the Philippines, or Vietnam, and that the United States could be drawn into such a crisis or conflict as a result of obligations the United States has under bilateral security treaties with Japan and the Philippines.

More broadly, China's actions for asserting and defending its maritime territorial and EEZ claims have led to increasing concerns among some observers that China may be seeking to dominate or gain control of its near-seas region, meaning the ECS, the SCS, and the Yellow Sea. Chinese domination over or control of this region, or Chinese actions that are perceived as being aimed at achieving such domination or control, could have major implications for the United States, including implications for U.S.-China relations, for interpreting China's rise as a major world power, for the security structure of the Asia-Pacific region, for the long-standing U.S. strategic goal of preventing the emergence of a regional hegemon in one part of Eurasia or another, and for two key elements of the U.S.-led international order that has operated since World War II—the non-use of force or coercion as a means of settling disputes between countries, and freedom of the seas.

China is a party to multiple territorial disputes in the SCS and ECS, including, in particular, disputes over the Paracel Islands, Spratly Islands, and Scarborough Shoal in the SCS, and the Senkaku Islands in the ECS. China depicts its territorial claims in the SCS using the so-called map of the nine-dash line that appears to enclose an area covering roughly 90% of the SCS. Some observers characterize China's approach for asserting and defending its territorial claims in the ECS and SCS as a "salami-slicing" strategy that employs a series of incremental actions, none of which by itself is a *casus belli*, to gradually change the status quo in China's favor. At least one Chinese official has used the term "cabbage strategy" to refer to a strategy of consolidating control over disputed islands by wrapping those islands, like the leaves of a cabbage, in successive layers of occupation and protection formed by fishing boats, Chinese Coast Guard ships, and then finally Chinese naval ships.

In addition to territorial disputes in the SCS and ECS, China is involved in a dispute, particularly with the United States, over whether China has a right under international law to regulate the activities of foreign military forces operating within China's EEZ. The dispute appears to be at the heart of incidents between Chinese and U.S. ships and aircraft in international waters and airspace in 2001, 2002, 2009, and 2013.

The U.S. position on territorial and EEZ disputes in the Western Pacific (including those involving China) includes the following elements, among others: The United States takes no position on competing claims to sovereignty over disputed land features in the ECS and SCS. Claims of territorial waters and EEZs should be consistent with customary international law of the sea and must therefore, among other things, derive from land features. Claims in the SCS that are not derived from land features are fundamentally flawed. Territorial disputes should be resolved peacefully, without coercion, intimidation, threats, or the use of force. Parties should avoid taking provocative or unilateral actions that disrupt the status quo or jeopardize peace and security; the Senkaku Islands are under the administration of Japan and unilateral attempts to change the status quo raise tensions and do nothing under international law to strengthen territorial claims. The United States has a national interest in the preservation of freedom of seas as recognized in customary international law of the sea. The United States opposes claims that impinge on the rights, freedoms, and lawful uses of the sea that belong to all nations. The United States, like most other countries, believes that coastal states under UNCLOS have the right to regulate economic activities in their EEZs, but do not have the right to regulate foreign military activities in their EEZs.

The situation concerning maritime territorial and EEZ disputes involving China raises several potential policy and oversight issues for Congress. Legislation in the 113th Congress concerning maritime territorial and EEZ disputes involving China in the SCS and ECS includes H.R. 4435/S. 2410 (the FY2015 National Defense Authorization Act), H.R. 4495, H.R. 772, S.Res. 412, and S.Res. 167.

Contents

Figures

Appendixes

Contacts

Introduction

China's actions for asserting and defending its maritime territorial and exclusive economic zone (EEZ)[1] claims in the East China (ECS) and South China Sea (SCS), particularly since late 2013, have heightened concerns among observers that ongoing disputes over these waters and some of the islands within them could lead to a crisis or conflict between China and a neighboring country such as Japan, the Philippines, or Vietnam, and that the United States could be drawn into such a crisis or conflict as a result of obligations the United States has under bilateral security treaties with Japan and the Philippines.

More broadly, China's actions for asserting and defending its maritime territorial and EEZ claims have led to increasing concerns among some observers that China may be seeking to dominate or gain control of its near-seas region, meaning the ECS, the SCS, and the Yellow Sea. Chinese domination over or control of this region, or Chinese actions that are perceived as being aimed at achieving such domination or control, could have major implications for the United States, including implications for U.S.-China relations, for interpreting China's rise as a major world power, for the security structure of the Asia-Pacific region, for the long-standing U.S. strategic goal of preventing the emergence of a regional hegemon in one part of Eurasia or another, and for two key elements of the U.S.-led international order that has operated since World War II—the non-use of force or coercion as a means of settling disputes between countries, and freedom of the seas.

The situation concerning maritime territorial and EEZ disputes involving China raises several potential policy and oversight issues for Congress. Decisions that Congress makes on these issues could substantially affect U.S. political and economic interests in the Asia-Pacific region and U.S. military operations in both the Asia-Pacific region and elsewhere.

The specifics of China's maritime territorial disputes with other countries are discussed in greater detail in other CRS reports.[2] Additional CRS reports cover other aspects of U.S. relations with China and other countries in the region.

Background

Overview of Disputes

Maritime Territorial Disputes

China is a party to multiple maritime territorial disputes in the SCS and ECS, including in particular the following (see **Figure 1** for locations of the island groups listed below):

---

[1] A country's EEZ includes waters extending up to 200 nautical miles from its land territory. Coastal states have the right under the United Nations Convention on the Law of the Sea (UNCLOS) to regulate foreign economic activities in their own EEZs. EEZs were established as a feature of international law by UNCLOS.

[2] CRS Report R42930, *Maritime Territorial Disputes in East Asia: Issues for Congress*, by Ben Dolven, Mark E. Manyin, and Shirley A. Kan CRS Report R42761, *Senkaku (Diaoyu/Diaoyutai) Islands Dispute: U.S. Treaty Obligations*, by Mark E. Manyin; and CRS Report RL33436, *Japan-U.S. Relations: Issues for Congress*, coordinated by Emma Chanlett-Avery.

- a dispute over the **Paracel Islands** in the SCS, which are claimed by China and Vietnam, and occupied by China;

- a dispute over the **Spratly Islands** in the SCS, which are claimed entirely by China, Taiwan, and Vietnam, and in part by the Philippines, Malaysia, and Brunei, and which are occupied in part by all these countries except Brunei;

- a dispute over **Scarborough Shoal** in the SCS, which is claimed by China, Taiwan, and the Philippines; and

- a dispute over the **Senkaku Islands** in the ECS, which are claimed by China, Taiwan, and Japan, and administered by Japan.

The island and shoal names used above are the ones commonly used in the United States; in other countries, these islands are known by various other names. China, for example, refers to the Paracel Islands as the Xisha islands, to the Spratly Islands as the Nansha islands, to Scarborough Shoal as Huangyan island, and to the Senkaku Islands as the Diaoyu islands.

These island groups are not the only land features in the SCS and ECS—the two seas feature other islands, rocks, shoals, and reefs, as well as some near-surface submerged features. The territorial status of some of these other features is also in dispute.[3] It should also be noted that there are additional maritime territorial disputes in the Western Pacific that do not involve China.[4]

Maritime territorial disputes in the SCS and ECS date back many years, and have periodically led to incidents and periods of increased tension.[5] The disputes have again intensified in the past few years, leading to numerous confrontations and incidents involving fishing vessels, oil exploration vessels and oil rigs, coast guard ships, naval ships, and military aircraft. The intensification of the disputes in recent years has substantially heightened tensions between China and other countries in the region, particularly Japan, the Philippines, and Vietnam.

---

[3] For example, the Reed Bank, a submerged atoll northeast of the Spratly Islands, is the subject of a dispute between China and the Philippines, and the Macclesfield Bank, a group of submerged shoals and reefs between the Paracel Islands and Scarborough Shoal, is claimed by China, Taiwan, and the Philippines. China refers to the Macclesfield Bank as the Zhongsha islands, even though they are submerged features rather than islands.

[4] North Korea and South Korea, for example, have not reached final agreement on their exact maritime border; South Korea and Japan are involved in a dispute over the Liancourt Rocks—a group of islets in the Sea of Japan that Japan refers to as the Takeshima islands and South Korea as the Dokdo islands; and Japan and Russia are involved in a dispute over islands dividing the Sea of Okhotsk from the Pacific Ocean that Japan refers to as the Northern Territories and Russia refers to as the South Kuril Islands.

[5] One observer states that "notable incidents over sovereignty include the Chinese attack on the forces of the Republic of Vietnam [South Vietnam] in the Paracel Islands in 1974, China's attack on Vietnamese forces near Fiery Cross Reef [in the Spratly Islands] in 1988, and China's military ouster of Philippines forces from Mischief Reef [also in the Spratly Islands] in 1995." Peter Dutton, "Three Dispute and Three Objectives," *Naval War College Review*, Autumn 2011: 43. A similar recounting can be found in Department of Defense, *Annual Report to Congress, Military and Security Developments Involving the People's Republic of China*, 2011, p. 15.

Figure 1. Maritime Territorial Disputes Involving China

Island groups involved in principal disputes

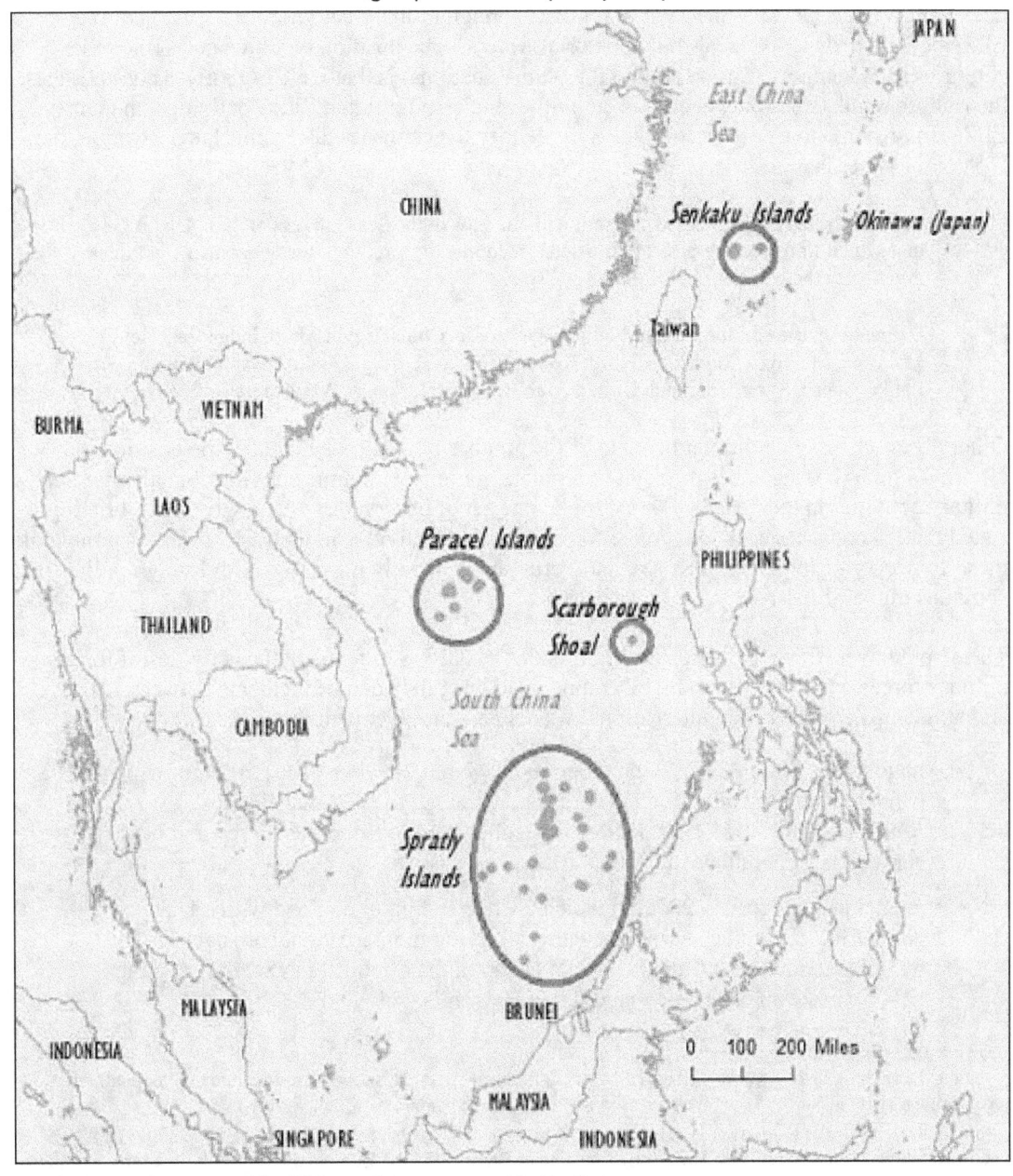

Source: Map prepared by CRS using base maps provided by Esri.

Note: Disputed islands have been enlarged to make them more visible.

Dispute Regarding China's Rights Within Its EEZ

In addition to maritime territorial disputes in the SCS and ECS, China is involved in a dispute, particularly with the United States, over whether China has a right under international law to regulate the activities of foreign military forces operating within China's EEZ. The position of the United States and most countries is that while the United Nations Convention on the Law of the

Sea (UNCLOS), which established EEZs as a feature of international law, gives coastal states the right to regulate economic activities (such as fishing and oil exploration) within their EEZs, it does not give coastal states the right to regulate foreign military activities in the parts of their EEZs beyond their 12-nautical-mile territorial waters.[6] The position of China and some other countries (i.e., a minority group among the world's nations) is that UNCLOS gives coastal states the right to regulate not only economic activities, but also foreign military activities, in their EEZs. In response to a request from CRS to identify the countries taking this latter position, the U.S. Navy states that

> countries with restrictions inconsistent with the Law of the Sea Convention [i.e., UNCLOS] that would limit the exercise of high seas freedoms by foreign navies beyond 12 nautical miles from the coast are [the following 27]:

> Bangladesh, Brazil, Burma, Cambodia, Cape Verde, China, Egypt, Haiti, India, Iran, Kenya, Malaysia, Maldives, Mauritius, North Korea, Pakistan, Portugal, Saudi Arabia, Somalia, Sri Lanka, Sudan, Syria, Thailand, United Arab Emirates, Uruguay, Venezuela, and Vietnam.[7]

Other observers provide different counts of the number of countries that take the position that UNCLOS gives coastal states the right to regulate not only economic activities but also foreign military activities in their EEZs. For example, one set of observers, in an August 2013 briefing, stated that 18 countries seek to regulate foreign military activities in their EEZs, and that three of these countries—China, North Korea, and Peru—have directly interfered with foreign military activities in their EEZs.[8]

The dispute over whether China has a right under UNCLOS to regulate the activities of foreign military forces operating within its EEZ appears to be at the heart of incidents between Chinese and U.S. ships and aircraft in international waters and airspace, including

- incidents in March 2001, September 2002, March 2009, and May 2009, in which Chinese ships and aircraft confronted and harassed the U.S. naval ships *Bowditch*, *Impeccable*, and *Victorious* as they were conducting survey and ocean surveillance operations in China's EEZ;

- an incident on April 1, 2001, in which a Chinese fighter collided with a U.S. Navy EP-3 electronic surveillance aircraft flying in international airspace about 65 miles southeast of China's Hainan Island in the South China Sea, forcing the EP-3 to make an emergency landing on Hainan Island;[9] and

---

[6] The legal term under UNCLOS for territorial waters is territorial seas. This report uses the more colloquial term territorial waters to avoid confusion with terms like South China Sea and East China Sea.

[7] Source: Navy Office of Legislative Affairs email to CRS, June 15, 2012. The email notes that two additional countries—Ecuador and Peru—also have restrictions inconsistent with UNCLOS that would limit the exercise of high seas freedoms by foreign navies beyond 12 nautical miles from the coast, but do so solely because they claim an extension of their territorial sea beyond 12 nautical miles.

[8] Source: Joe Baggett and Pete Pedrozo, briefing for Center for Naval Analysis Excessive Chinese Maritime Claims Workshop, August 7, 2013, slide entitled "What are other nations' views?" (slide 30 of 47). The slide also notes that there have been "isolated diplomatic protests from Pakistan, India, and Brazil over military surveys" conducted in their EEZs.

[9] For discussions of some of these incidents and their connection to the issue of military operating rights in EEZs, see Raul Pedrozo, "Close Encounters at Sea, The USNS Impeccable Incident," *Naval War College Review*, Summer 2009: 101-111; Jonathan G. Odom, "The True 'Lies' of the *Impeccable* Incident: What Really Happened, Who Disregarded International Law, and Why Every Nation (Outside of China) Should Be Concerned," *Michigan State Journal of* (continued...)

- an incident on December 5, 2013, in which a Chinese navy ship put itself in the path of the U.S. Navy cruiser *Cowpens* as it was operating 30 or more miles from China's aircraft carrier *Liaoning*, forcing the *Cowpens* to change course to avoid a collision.

Figure 2 shows the locations of the 2001, 2002, and 2009 incidents listed in the first two bullets above. The incidents shown in **Figure 2** are the ones most commonly cited prior to the December 2013 involving the *Cowpens*, but some observers list additional incidents as well. For example, one set of observers, in an August 2013 briefing, provided the following list of incidents in which China has challenged or interfered with operations by U.S. ships and aircraft and ships from India's navy:

- USNS *Bowditch* (March 2001);

- EP-3 Incident (April 2001);

- USNS *Impeccable* (March 2009);

- USNS *Victorious* (May 2009);

- USS *George Washington* (July-November 2010);

- U-2 Intercept (June 2011);

- INS [Indian Naval Ship] *Airavat* (July 2011);

- INS [Indian Naval Ship] *Shivalik* (June 2012); and

- USNS *Impeccable* (July 2013).[10]

Regarding some of these incidents, one observer states that

> the airmen and sailors of all countries know how to operate around each other in a safe fashion. There is no lack of knowledge or training. The rules are well understood as to how you operate your ship or your airplane so you don't hit somebody.
>
> What matters is the political direction given to the military. If your government says to you, "I really want you to muscle those people. Forget about the rules. Just see if you can make them give way." That's what led to the incident in 2001. That's what led to the incident with

---

(...continued)

International Law, vol. 18, no. 3, 2010: 16-22, accessed September 25, 2012, at http://papers.ssrn.com/sol3/ papers.cfm?abstract_id=1622943; Oriana Skylar Mastro, "Signaling and Military Provocation in Chinese National Security Strategy: A Closer Look at the Impeccable Incident," *Journal of Strategic Studies*, April 2011: 219-244; and Peter Dutton, ed., *Military Activities in the EEZ, A U.S.-China Dialogue on Security and International Law in the Maritime Commons*, Newport (RI), Naval War College, China Maritime Studies Institute, China Maritime Study Number 7, December 2010, 124 pp. See also CRS Report RL30946, *China-U.S. Aircraft Collision Incident of April 2001: Assessments and Policy Implications*, by Shirley A. Kan et al.

[10] Source: Joe Baggett and Pete Pedrozo, briefing for Center for Naval Analysis Excessive Chinese Maritime Claims Workshop, August 7, 2013, slide entitled "Notable EEZ Incidents with China," (slides 37 and 46 of 47). Regarding an event involving the *Impeccable* reported to have taken place in June rather than July, see William Cole, "Chinese Help Plan For Huge War Game Near Isles," Honolulu Star-Advertiser, July 25, 2013: 1. See also Bill Gertz, "Inside the Ring: New Naval Harassment in Asia," July 17, 2013. See also Department of Defense Press Briefing by Adm. Locklear in the Pentagon Briefing Room, July 11, 2013, accessed August 9, 2013, at http://www.defense.gov/ transcripts/transcript.aspx?transcriptid=5270.

the USS Cowpens in the South China Sea last December when the Chinese ship cut in front of it.[11]

Figure 2. Locations of 2001, 2002, and 2009 U.S.-Chinese Incidents at Sea and In Air

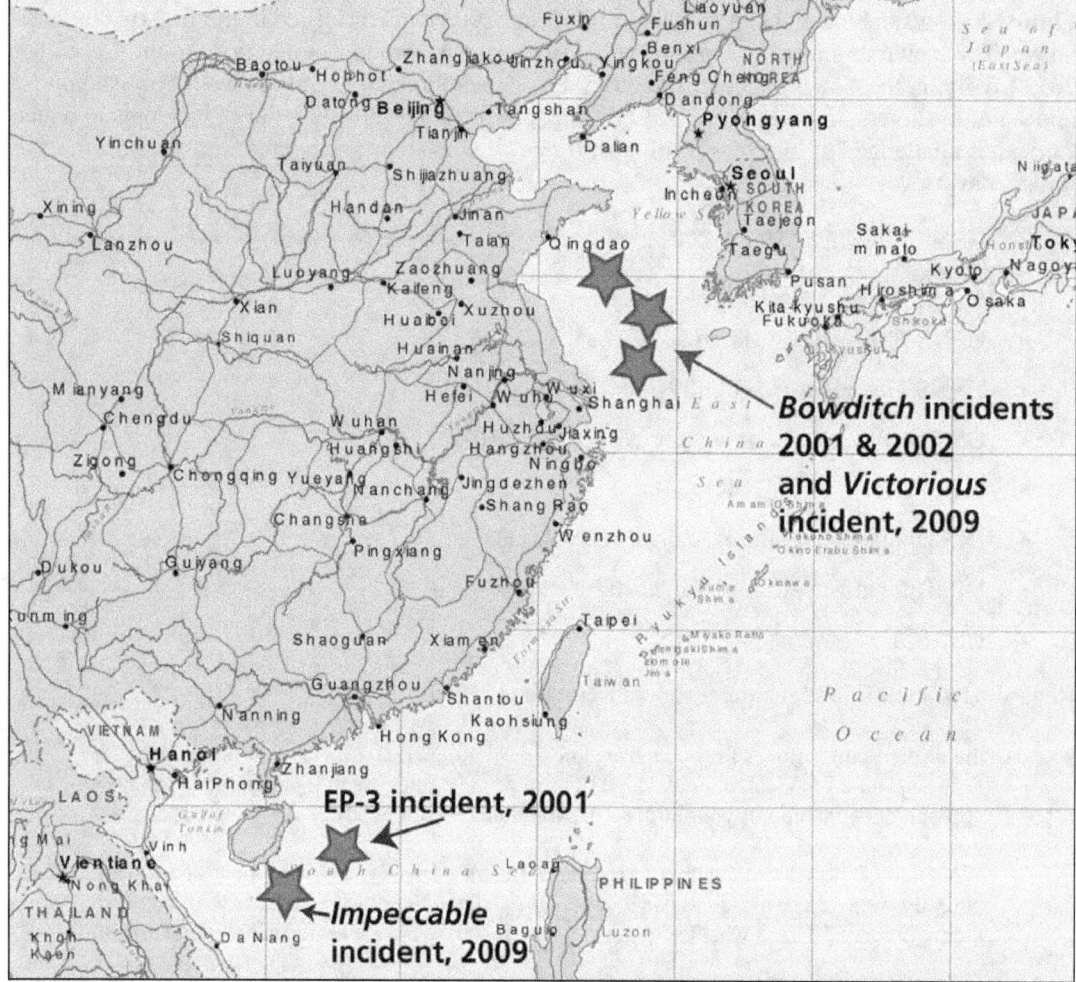

Source: Mark E. Redden and Phillip C. Saunders, *Managing Sino-U.S. Air and Naval Interactions: Cold War Lessons and New Avenues of Approach*, Washington, Center for the Study of Chinese Military Affairs, Institute for National Strategic Studies, National Defense University, September 2012. Detail of map shown on page 6.

Relationship of Maritime Territorial Disputes to EEZ Dispute

The issue of whether China has the right under UNCLOS to regulate foreign military activities in its EEZ is related to, but ultimately separate from, the issue of territorial disputes in the SCS and ECS. The two issues are related because China can claim EEZs from inhabitable islands over which it has sovereignty, so accepting China's claims to sovereignty over inhabitable islands in

---

[11] Yoichi Kato, "Interview: Dennis Blair: China Containing Itself By Aggressive Actions In Region," *Asahi Shimbun* (*http://ajw.asahi.com*), June 26, 2014.

the SCS or ECS could permit China to expand the EEZ zone within which China claims a right to regulate foreign military activities.

The EEZ issue is ultimately separate from the territorial disputes issue because even if all the territorial disputes in the SCS and ECS were resolved, and none of China's claims in the SCS and ECS were accepted, China could continue to apply its concept of its EEZ rights to the EEZ that it unequivocally derives from its mainland coast—and it is in this unequivocal Chinese EEZ that most of the past U.S.-Chinese incidents at sea have occurred.

Press reports of maritime disputes in the SCS and ECS often focus on territorial disputes while devoting little or no attention to the related but ultimately separate EEZ dispute. From the U.S. perspective, however, the EEZ dispute is arguably as significant as the maritime territorial disputes because of its potential for leading to a U.S.-Chinese incident at sea[12] and because of its potential for affecting U.S. military operations not only in the SCS and ECS, but around the world.

1972 Multilateral Convention on Preventing Collisions at Sea (COLREGs Convention)

China and the United States, as well as more than 150 other countries (including all those bordering on the South East and South China Seas other than Taiwan),[13] are parties to an October 1972 multilateral convention on international regulations for preventing collisions at sea, commonly known as the collision regulations (COLREGs) or the "rules of the road."[14] Although referred to as a set of rules or regulations, the multilateral convention is a binding treaty. The convention applies "to all vessels upon the high seas and in all waters connected therewith navigable by seagoing vessels."[15]

In a February 18, 2014, letter to Senator Marco Rubio concerning the December 5, 2013, incident involving the *Cowpens*, the State Department stated:

> In order to minimize the potential for an accident or incident at sea, it is important that the United States and China share a common understanding of the rules for operational air or maritime interactions. From the U.S. perspective, an existing body of international rules and guidelines—including the 1972 International Regulations for Preventing Collisions at Sea (COLREGs)—are sufficient to ensure the safety of navigation between U.S. forces and the force of other countries, including China. We will continue to make clear to the Chinese that these existing rules, including the COLREGs, should form the basis for our common

---

[12] For a discussion, see Jeff M. Smith and Joshua Eisenman, "China and America Clash on the High Seas: The EEZ Challenge," *The National Interest* (http://nationalinterest.org), May 22, 2014.

[13] Source: International Maritime Organization, *Status of Multilateral Conventions and Instruments in Respect of Which the International Maritime Organization or its Secretary-General Performs Depositary or Other Functions, As at 28 February 2014*, pp. 86-89. The Philippines acceded to the convention on June 10, 2013.

[14] 28 UST 3459; TIAS 8587. The treaty was done at London October 20, 1972, and entered into force July 15, 1977. The United States is an original signatory to the convention and acceded the convention entered into force for the United States on July 15, 1977. China acceded to the treaty on January 7, 1980. A summary of the agreement is available at http://www.imo.org/About/Conventions/ListOfConventions/Pages/COLREG.aspx. The text of the convention is available at https://treaties.un.org/doc/Publication/UNTS/Volume%201050/volume-1050-I-15824-English.pdf.

[15] Rule 1(a) of the convention.

understanding of air and maritime behavior, and we will encourage China to incorporate these rules into its incident-management tools.

Likewise, we will continue to urge China to agree to adopt bilateral crisis management tools with Japan and to rapidly conclude negotiations with ASEAN[16] on a robust and meaningful Code of Conduct in the South China in order to avoid incidents and to manage them when they arise. We will continue to stress the importance of these issues in our regular interactions with Chinese officials.[17]

In the 2014 edition of its annual report on military and security developments involving China, the Department of Defense (DOD) states:

On December 5, 2013, a PLA Navy vessel and a U.S. Navy vessel operating in the South China Sea came into close proximity. At the time of the incident, USS COWPENS (CG 63) was operating approximately 32 nautical miles southeast of Hainan Island. In that location, the U.S. Navy vessel was conducting lawful military activities beyond the territorial sea of any coastal State, consistent with customary international law as reflected in the Law of the Sea Convention. Two PLA Navy vessels approached USS COWPENS. During this interaction, one of the PLA Navy vessels altered course and crossed directly in front of the bow of USS COWPENS. This maneuver by the PLA Navy vessel forced USS COWPENS to come to full stop to avoid collision, while the PLA Navy vessel passed less than 100 yards ahead. The PLA Navy vessel's action was inconsistent with internationally recognized rules concerning professional maritime behavior (i.e., the Convention of International Regulations for Preventing Collisions at Sea), to which China is a party.[18]

2014 Code For Unplanned Encounters At Sea (CUES)

On April 22, 2014, representatives of 21 Pacific-region navies (including China, Japan, and the United States), meeting in Qingdao, China, at the 14th Western Pacific Naval Symposium (WPNS),[19] unanimously agreed to a Code for Unplanned Encounters at Sea (CUES). CUES, a

---

[16] ASEAN is the Association of Southeast Asian Nations. ASEAN's member states are Brunei, Cambodia, Indonesia, Laos, Malaysia, Myanmar, the Philippines, Singapore, Thailand, and Vietnam.

[17] Letter dated February 18, 2014, from Julia Frifield, Assistant Secretary, Legislative Affairs, Department of State, to The Honorable Marco Rubio, United States Senate. Used here with the permission of the office of Senator Rubio. The letter begins: "Thank you for your letter of January 31 regarding the December 5, 2013, incident involving a Chinese naval vessel and the USS Cowpens." The text of Senator Rubio's January 31, 2014, letter was accessed March 13, 2014, at http://www.rubio.senate.gov/public/index.cfm/2014/1/rubio-calls-on-administration-to-address-provocative-chinese-behavior.

[18] Department of Defense, *Annual Report to Congress [on] Military and Security Developments Involving the People's Republic of China 2014*, p. 4.

[19] As described in one press release, the WPNS

> The Western Pacific Naval Symposium (WPNS) comprises navies whose countries border the Pacific Ocean region. It was inaugurated in 1988 after navy chiefs attending the International Seapower Symposium in 1987 agreed to establish a forum where leaders of regional navies could meet to discuss cooperative initiatives. Under the WPNS, member countries convene biennially to discuss regional and global maritime issues.

> As of October 2010, WPNS membership stands at 20 members and four observers. They are:

> Members: Australia, Brunei, Cambodia, Canada, Chile, France, Indonesia, Japan, Malaysia, New Zealand, Papua New Guinea, People's Republic of China, Philippines, Republic of Korea, Russia, Singapore, Thailand, Tonga, United States of America and Vietnam

> Observers: Bangladesh, India, Mexico and Peru

(continued...)

---

non-binding agreement, establishes a standardized protocol of safety procedures, basic communications and basic maneuvering instructions for naval ships and aircraft during unplanned encounters at sea, with the aim of reducing the risk of incidents arising from such encounters.[20]

Two observers stated that "The resolution is non-binding; only regulates communication in 'unplanned encounters,' not behavior; fails to address incidents in territorial waters; and does not apply to fishing and maritime constabulary vessels, which are responsible for the majority of Chinese harassment operations."[21] An April 23, 2014, press report stated:

> Beijing won't necessarily observe a new code of conduct for naval encounters when its ships meet foreign ones in disputed areas of the East and South China seas, according to a senior Chinese naval officer involved in negotiations on the subject....
>
> U.S. naval officers have said they hoped all members of the group would observe the code in all places, including waters where China's territorial claims are contested by its neighbors.
>
> But the code isn't legally binding, and it remains to be seen whether China will observe it in what the U.S. sees as international waters and Beijing sees as part of its territory.
>
> Senior Capt. Ren Xiaofeng, the head of the Chinese navy's Maritime Security/Safety Policy Research Division, said that when and where the code was implemented had to be discussed bilaterally between China and other nations, including the U.S.
>
> "It's recommended, not legally binding," Capt. Ren told The Wall Street Journal....[22]

Another observer states that China

> touts the fact that it recently signed a Code for Unplanned Encounters at Sea at the recent Western Pacific Naval Symposium held in Qingdao. CUES is meant to help avoid accidents at sea. However, the code is voluntary and applies only when naval ships and aircraft meet "casually or unexpectedly." It also does not apply to a country's territorial waters, and of

---

(...continued)

    (Singapore Ministry of Defense, "Fact Sheet: Background of the Western Pacific Naval Symposium, MCMEX, DIVEX and NMS," updated March 25, 2011, accessed October 1, 2012, at http://www.mindef.gov.sg/imindef/news_and_events/nr/2011/mar/25mar11_nr/25mar11_fs html. See also the website for the 2012 WPNS at http://www.navy.mil my/wpns2012/.)

[20] See, for example, "Navy Leaders Agree to CUES at 14th WPNS," Navy News Services, April 23, 2014; Austin Ramzy and Chris Buckley, "Pacific Rim Deal Could Reduce Chance of Unintended Conflict in Contested Seas," *New York Times (www.nytimes.com)*, April 23, 2014; Megha Rajagopalan, "Pacific Accord on Maritime Code Could Help Prevent Conflicts," *Reuters.com*, April 22, 104.

For additional background information on CUES, see Mark E. Redden and Phillip C. Saunders, *Managing Sino-U.S. Air and Naval Interactions: Cold War Lessons and New Avenues of Approach*, Washington, Center for the Study of Chinese Military Affairs, Institute for National Strategic Studies, National Defense University, September 2012, pp. 8-9. The text of the previous 2003 CUES Review Supplement was accessed October 1, 2012, at http://navy mil.my/wpns2012/images/stories/dokumen/WPNS%202012%20PRESENTATION%20FOLDER/ACTION%20ITEMS%20WPNS%20WORKSHOP%202012/CUES.PDF.

[21] Jeff M. Smith and Joshua Eisenman, "China and America Clash on the High Seas: The EEZ Challenge," *The National Interest (*http://nationalinterest.org*)*, May 22, 2014.

[22] Jeremy Page, "China Won't Necessarily Observe New Conduct Code for Navies," *Wall Street Journal (*http://online.wsj.com*)*, April 23, 2014.

---

course countering China's expansive claims to territorial waters is one of the most pressing problems in the South and East China Seas.[23]

Negotiations Between China and ASEAN on SCS Code of Conduct

In 2002, China and the 10 member states of ASEAN signed a non-binding Declaration on the Conduct (DOC) of Parties in the South China Sea in which the parties, among other things,

> ... reaffirm their respect for and commitment to the freedom of navigation in and overflight above the South China Sea as provided for by the universally recognized principles of international law, including the 1982 UN Convention on the Law of the Sea....

> ... undertake to resolve their territorial and jurisdictional disputes by peaceful means, without resorting to the threat or use of force, through friendly consultations and negotiations by sovereign states directly concerned, in accordance with universally recognized principles of international law, including the 1982 UN Convention on the Law of the Sea....

> ... undertake to exercise self-restraint in the conduct of activities that would complicate or escalate disputes and affect peace and stability including, among others, refraining from action of inhabiting on the presently uninhabited islands, reefs, shoals, cays, and other features and to handle their differences in a constructive manner....

> .. reaffirm that the adoption of a [follow-on] code of conduct in the South China Sea would further promote peace and stability in the region and agree to work, on the basis of consensus, towards the eventual attainment of this objective....[24]

In July 2011, China and ASEAN adopted a preliminary set of principles for implementing the DOC. U.S. officials since 2010 have encouraged ASEAN and China to develop the follow-on binding Code of Conduct (COC) mentioned in the final paragraph above. China and ASEAN have conducted negotiations on the follow-on COC, but China has not yet agreed with the ASEAN member states on a final text. An August 5, 2013, press report states that "China is in no rush to sign a proposed agreement on maritime rules with Southeast Asia governing behavior in the disputed South China Sea, and countries should not have unrealistic expectations, the Chinese foreign minister said on Monday [August 5]."[25]

China's Approach to Maritime Territorial Disputes

Map of the Nine-Dash Line

China depicts its territorial claims in the SCS using the so-called map of the nine-dash line—a Chinese map of the SCS showing nine line segments that, if connected, would enclose an area covering roughly 90% (earlier estimates said about 80%) of the SCS (**Figure 3**).

---

[23] Patrick Cronin, "China's Problem With Rules: Managing A Reluctant Stakeholder," War on the Rocks (http://warontherocks.com), June 26, 2014.

[24] For the full text of the declaration, see **Appendix B**.

[25] Ben Blanchard, "China Says In No Hurry to Sign South China Sea Accord," *Reuters.com*, August 5, 2013. See also Shannon Tiezzi, "Why China Isn't Interested in a South China Sea Code of Conduct," *The Diplomat* (http://thediplomat.com), February 26, 2014.

Figure 3. Map of the Nine-Dash Line

Example submitted by China to the United Nations in 2009

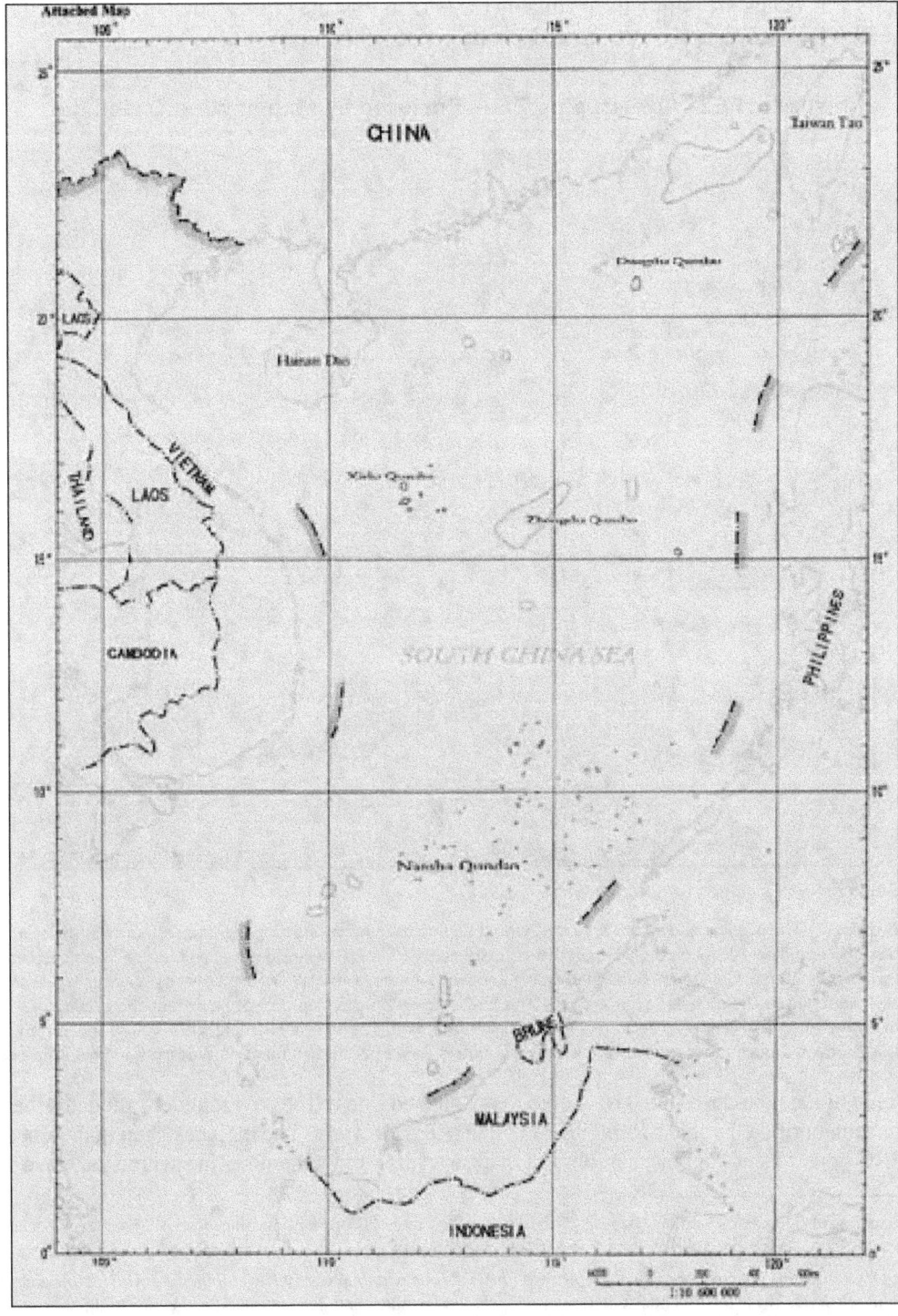

Source: Communication from China to the United Nations dated May 7, 2009, English version, accessed on August 30, 2012, at http://www.un.org/Depts/los/clcs_new/submissions_files/submission_vnm_37_2009.htm.

The area inside the nine line segments far exceeds what is claimable as territorial waters under customary international law of the sea as reflected in UNCLOS, and, as shown in **Figure 4**, includes waters that are within the claimable EEZs (and in some places are quite near the coasts) of the Philippines, Malaysia, Brunei, and Vietnam.

Figure 4. EEZs Overlapping Zone Enclosed by Map of Nine-Dash Line

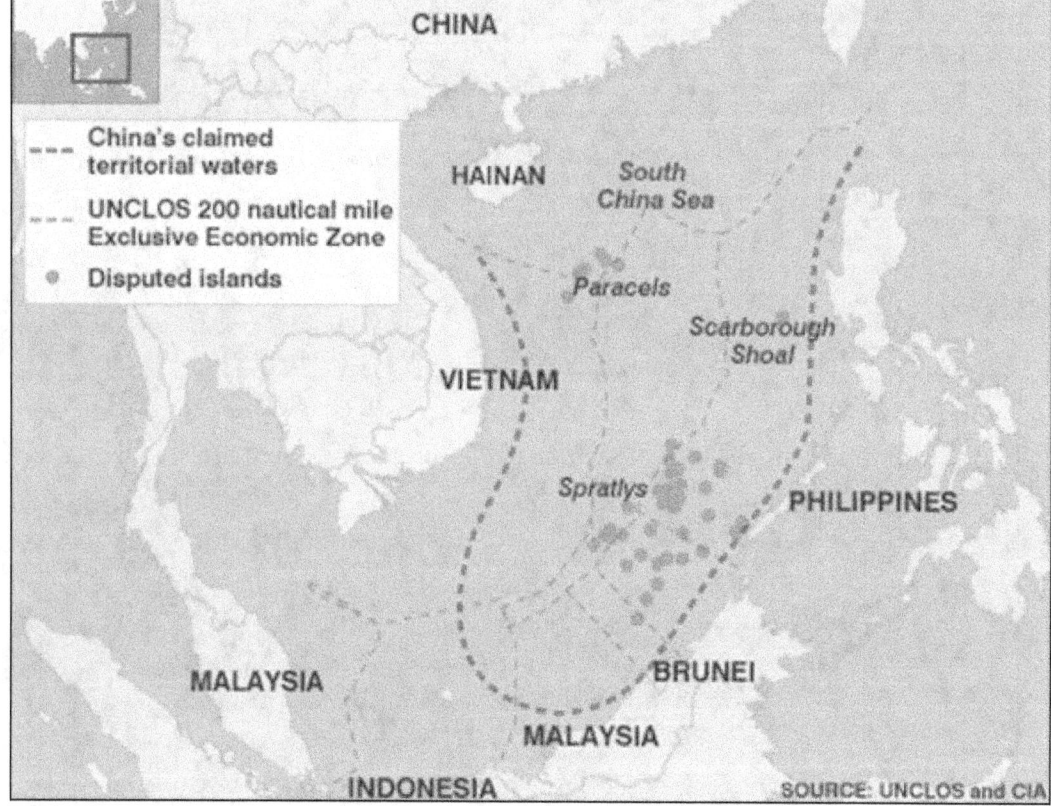

Source: Source: Eurasia Review, September 10, 2012.

Notes: (1) The red line shows the area that would be enclosed by connecting the line segments in the map of the nine-dash line. Although the label on this map states that the waters inside the red line are "China's claimed territorial waters," China has maintained ambiguity over whether it is claiming full sovereignty over the entire area enclosed by the nine line segments. (2) The EEZs shown on the map do not represent the totality of maritime territorial claims by countries in the region. Vietnam, to cite one example, claims all of the Spratly Islands, even though most or all of the islands are outside the EEZ that Vietnam derives from its mainland coast.

The map of the nine-dash line, also called the U-shaped line or the cow tongue,[26] predates the establishment of the People's Republic of China (PRC) in 1949. The map has been maintained by the PRC government, and maps published in Taiwan also show the nine line segments.[27] In a

---

[26] The map is also sometimes called the map of the nine dashed lines (as opposed to nine-dash line), perhaps because some maps (such as **Figure 3**) show each line segment as being dashed.

[27] See Department of Defense, *Annual Report to Congress, Military and Security Developments Involving the People's Republic of China*, 2011, pp. 15 and 39; Peter Dutton, "Three Disputes and Three Objectives, China and the South China Sea," *Naval War College Review*, Autumn 2011: 44-45; Hong Nong, "Interpreting the U-shape Line in the South China, Sea," accessed on September 28, 2012, at http://chinausfocus.com/peace-security/interpreting-the-u-shape-line-in-the-south-china-sea/.

document submitted to the United Nations on May 7, 2009, that included the map as an attachment, China stated:

> China has indisputable sovereignty over the islands in the South China Sea and the adjacent waters, and enjoys sovereign rights and jurisdiction over the relevant waters as well as the seabed and subsoil thereof (see attached map [of the nine-dash line]). The above position is consistently held by the Chinese Government, and is widely known by the international community.[28]

The map does not always have exactly nine dashes. Early versions of the map had as many as 11 dashes, and a new map of China published by the Chinese government in June 2014 includes 10 dashes.[29]

China has maintained some ambiguity over whether it is using the map of the nine-dash line to claim full sovereignty over the entire sea area enclosed by the nine-dash line, or something less than that.[30] Maintaining this ambiguity can be viewed as an approach that preserves flexibility for China in pursuing its maritime claims in the SCS while making it more difficult for other parties to define specific objections or pursue legal challenges to those claims. It does appear clear, however, that China at a minimum claims sovereignty over the island groups inside the nine line segments—China's domestic Law on the Territorial Sea and Contiguous Zone, enacted in 1992, specifies that China claims sovereignty over all the island groups inside the nine line segments.[31] China's implementation on January 1, 2014, of a series of fishing regulations covering much of the SCS suggests that China claims at least some degree of administrative control over much of the SCS.

"Salami-Slicing" Strategy and "Cabbage" Strategy

Some observers characterize China's approach for asserting and defending its territorial claims in the ECS and SCS as a "salami-slicing" strategy that employs a series of incremental actions, none of which by itself is a *casus belli*, to gradually change the status quo in China's favor.[32] At least

---

[28] Communication from China to the United Nations dated May 7, 2009, English version, accessed on August 30, 2012, at http://www.un.org/Depts/los/clcs_new/submissions_files/submission_vnm_37_2009 htm.

[29] For an article discussing this map in general (but not that it includes 10 dashes), see Ben Blanchard and Sui-Lee Wee, "New Chinese Map Gives Greater Play to South China Sea Claims," *Reuters (www.reuters.com)*, June 25, 2014.

[30] See Andrew Browne, "China's line in the Sea," *Wall Street Journal* (http://online.wsj.com), April 1, 2014; Peter Dutton, "Three Disputes and Three Objectives, China and the South China Sea," *Naval War College Review*, Autumn 2011: 45-48; Hong Nong, "Interpreting the U-shape Line in the South China, Sea," accessed September 28, 2012, at http://chinausfocus.com/peace-security/interpreting-the-u-shape-line-in-the-south-china-sea/.) See also Ankit Panda, "Will China's Nine Dashes Ever Turn Into One Line?" *The Diplomat (http://thediplomat.com)*, July 1, 2014.

[31] Peter Dutton, "Three Disputes and Three Objectives, China and the South China Sea," *Naval War College Review*, Autumn 2011: 45, which states: "In 1992, further clarifying its claims of sovereignty over all the islands in the South China Sea, the People's Republic of China enacted its Law on the Territorial Sea and Contiguous Zone, which specifies that China claims sovereignty over the features of all of the island groups that fall within the U-shaped line in the South China Sea: the Pratas Islands (Dongsha), the Paracel Islands (Xisha), Macclesfield Bank (Zhongsha), and the Spratly Islands (Nansha)." See also International Crisis Group, *Stirring Up the South China Sea ([Part] I)*, Asia Report Number 223, April 23, 2012, pp. 3-4.

[32] See, for example, Statement before the U.S. House Armed Services [Committee,] Subcommittee on Seapower and Projection Forces and the House Foreign Affairs [Committee,] Subcommittee on the Asia Pacific [sic: Asia and the Pacific] [on] "People's Republic of China Maritime Disputes," A Statement by Bonnie S. Glaser, Senior Adviser, Freeman Chair in China Studies, Center for Strategic and International Studies (CSIS), January 14, 2014, pp. 3-5; Robert Haddick, "Getting Tough in the South China Sea," *National Interest* (http://nationalinterest.org), February 25, (continued...)

one Chinese official has used the term "cabbage strategy" to refer to a strategy of consolidating control over disputed islands by wrapping those islands, like the leaves of a cabbage, in successive layers of occupation and protection formed by fishing boats, Chinese Coast Guard ships, and then finally Chinese naval ships.[33] Other observers have referred to China's approach as a strategy of creeping annexation[34] or as a "talk and take" strategy, meaning a strategy in which China engages in (or draws out) negotiations while taking actions to gain control of contested areas.[35]

Use of China Coast Guard Ships and Other Ships

China makes regular use of China Coast Guard ships to assert and defend its maritime territorial claims, with Chinese Navy ships sometimes available over the horizon as backup forces.[36]

(...continued)

2014; Robert Haddick, "America Has No Answer to China's Salami-Slicing," *War on the Rocks* (http://warontherocks.com), February 6, 2014.

[33] See Harry Kazianis, "China's Expanding Cabbage Strategy," *The Diplomat* (*http:thediplomat.com*), October 29, 2013; Bonnie S. Glaser and Alison Szalwinski, "Second Thomas Shoal Likely the Next Flashpoint in the South China Sea," *China Brief*, June 21, 2013, accessed August 9, 2013, at http://www.jamestown.org/programs/chinabrief/single/? tx_ttnews%5Btt_news%5D=41054&tx_ttnews%5BbackPid%5D=25&cHash= 6580ce14cee5ac00501d5439f3ee3632#.UdBFf8u9KSM; and Rafael M. Alunan III, "China's Cabbage Strategy," *Business World* (*Manila;* http://www.bworldonline.com), July 8, 2013. See also Loida Nicolas Lewis, Rodel Rodis, and Walden Bello, "China's 'Cabbage Strategy' in West PH Sea," *Philippine Daily Inquirer*, July 27, 2013.

[34] See, for example, Alan Dupont, "China's Maritime Power Trip," *The Australian*, May 24, 2014.

[35] See, for example, Patrick M. Cronin, et al, *Cooperation from Strength, The United States, China and the South China Sea*, Center for a New American Security, January 2012, pp. 16, 56, and 65 (note 19); David Brown, "China, Vietnam Drift in South China Sea," *Asia Times Online (www.atimes.com)*, January 21, 2012; Derek Bolton, "Pivoting Toward the South China Sea?" *Foreign Policy In Focus (*http://fpif.org*)*, June 11, 2012; John Lee, "China's Salami-slicing Is Dicey Diplomacy," *Hudson Institute (*http://hudson.org*)*, November 27, 2013; Fernando Fajardo, "Asia and the US Interest," Cebu Daily News (http://cebudailynews.inquirer net), April 16, 2014; Jacqueline Newmyer Deal, "Chinese Dominance Isn't Certain," *The National Interest (*http://nationalinterest.org*)*, April 22, 2014; David Brown, "Viets Gamble Vainly on Appeasement in South China Sea," *Asia Sentinel (www.asiasentinel.com)*, May 7, 2014.

[36] The Department of Defense (DOD) states:

> During the 2012 Scarborough Reef and 2013 Senkaku Islands tensions, the China Maritime Surveillance (CMS) and Fisheries Law Enforcement Command (FLEC) ships were responsible for directly asserting Chinese sovereignty on a daily basis, while the PLA Navy maintained a more distant presence from the immediate vicinity of the contested waters. China prefers to use its civilian maritime agencies around these islands, and uses the PLA Navy in a back-up role or as an escalatory measure. China's diplomats also apply pressure on rival claimants. China identifies its territorial sovereignty as a core interest and emphasizes its willingness to protect against actions that China perceives challenge Chinese sovereignty. China almost certainly wants to assert its maritime dominance without triggering too harsh of a regional backlash.

> In 2013, China consolidated four of its maritime law enforcement agencies into the China Coast Guard (CCG). Subordinate to the Ministry of Public Security, the CCG is responsible for a wide range of missions, including maritime sovereignty enforcement missions, anti-smuggling, maritime rescue and salvage, protecting fisheries resources, and general law enforcement. Prior to the consolidation, different agencies were responsible for each of these mission sets, creating organizational redundancies and complicating interagency coordination.

> In the next decade, a new force of civilian maritime ships will afford China the capability to patrol its territorial claims more robustly in the East China and the South China Seas. China is continuing with the second half of a modernization and construction program for the CCG. The first half of this program, from 2004 to 2008, resulted in the addition of almost 20 ocean-going patrol ships. The second half of this program, from 2011 to 2015, includes at least 30 new ships for the CCG. Several less capable patrol ships will be decommissioned during this period. In addition, the CCG

(continued...)

Chinese Coast Guard ships are unarmed or lightly armed, but can be effective in asserting and defending maritime territorial claims, particularly in terms of confronting or harassing foreign vessels that are similarly lightly armed or unarmed.[37] In addition to being available as backups for China Coast Guard ships, Chinese navy ships conduct exercises that in some cases appear intended, at least in part, at reinforcing China's maritime claims.[38] Some observers believe China also uses civilian fishing ships to assert and defend its maritime claims.[39]

Preference for Treating Disputes on Bilateral Basis

China prefers to discuss maritime territorial disputes with other parties to the disputes on a bilateral rather than multilateral basis. Some observers believe China prefers bilateral talks because China is much larger than any other country in the region, giving China a potential upper hand in any bilateral meeting. China generally has resisted multilateral approaches to resolving maritime territorial disputes, stating that such approaches would internationalize the disputes, although the disputes are by definition international even when addressed on a bilateral basis. (China's participation with the ASEAN states in the 2002 DOC and in negotiations with the ASEAN states on the follow-on binding code of conduct represents a departure from this general preference.) As noted above, some observers believe China is pursuing a policy of putting off a negotiated resolution of maritime territorial disputes so as to give itself time to implement the salami-slicing strategy.[40] China has resisted U.S. involvement in the disputes.[41]

(...continued)

will likely build more than 100 new patrol craft and smaller units, both to increase capability and to replace old units. Overall, The CCG's total force level is expected to increase by 25 percent. Some of these ships will have the capability to embark helicopters, a capability that only a few MLE [maritime law enforcement] ships currently have. The enlargement and modernization of China's MLE forces will improve China's ability to enforce its maritime sovereignty.

(Department of Defense, *Annual Report to Congress [on] Military and Security Developments Involving the People's Republic of China 2014*, p. 38.)

[37] See, for example, Megha Rajagopalan and Greg Torode, "China's Civilian Fleet A Potent Force in Asia's Disputed Waters," *Reuters.com*, March 5, 2014.

[38] See, for example, Trefor Moss and Rob Taylor, "Chinese Naval Patrol Pompts Conflicting Regional Response," *Wall Street Journal* (http://online.wsj.com), February 20, 2014.

[39] See James R. Holmes. *A Competitive Turn: How Increased Chinese Maritime Actions Complicate U.S. Partnerships*, Washington, Center for a New American Security, December 2012, East and South China Sea Bulletin 7, p. 1, accessed March 25, 2012, at http://www.cnas.org/files/documents/flashpoints/CNAS_bulletin_Holmes_ACompetitiveTurn.pdf; James R. Holmes, "China's Small Stick Diplomacy," *The Diplomat* (http://thediplomat.com), May 21, 2012, accessed October 3, 2012, at http://thediplomat.com/2012/05/21/chinas-small-stick-diplomacy/; Jens Kastner, "China's Fishermen Charge Enemy Lines," *Asia Times Online* (www.atimes.com), May 16, 2012; Carlyle A. Thayer, "Paracel Island: Chinese Boats Attack Vietnamese Fishing Craft," Thayer Consultancy Background Brief, May 28, 2013, p. 1.

[40] One observer, for example, states that "implementing the DOC, let alone transitioning to a COC, has proven chimerical. China is not the sole cause of delay; ASEAN is divided as to what, if anything, to do. But China's strategy is clear: to use fruitless diplomacy to buy time for factual primacy, thereby ensuring that future negotiations will serve Chinese ends." (Donald K. Emmerson, "China Challenges Philippines in the South China Sea," *East Asia Forum* (www.eastasiaforum.org), March 18, 2014.)

[41] For additional discussion of China's approach to maritime territorial disputes, see Patrick Cronin, "China's Problem With Rules: Managing A Reluctant Stakeholder," *War on the Rocks (http://warontherocks.com)*, June 26, 2014.

Comparison with U.S. Actions Toward Caribbean and Gulf of Mexico

Some observers have compared China's approach toward its near-seas region with the U.S. approach toward the Caribbean and the Gulf of Mexico in the age of the Monroe Doctrine. One observer, for example, states:

> Beijing is attempting to do in the East and South China Seas in the early twenty-first century what the United States successfully accomplished in the Greater Caribbean in the nineteenth and early-twentieth centuries. It has attempted to take effective strategic control of the blue water extension of its own continental land mass.[42]

It can be noted, however, that there are significant differences between China's approach to its near-seas region and the U.S. approach—both in the 19th and 20th Centuries and today—to the Caribbean and the Gulf of Mexico. Unlike China in its approach to its near-seas region, the United States has not asserted any form of sovereignty or historical rights over the broad waters of the Caribbean or Gulf of Mexico (or other sea areas beyond the 12-mile limit of U.S. territorial waters), has not published anything akin to the nine-dash line for these waters (or other sea areas beyond the 12-mile limit), and does not contest the right of foreign naval forces to operate and engage in various activities in waters beyond the 12-mile limit. One observer states:

> Chinese interlocutors are forever trying to use facile comparisons with U.S. history to get Americans to commit to unilateral intellectual disarmament. If we did it in the Caribbean then, how can we object when China does it in Southeast Asia now?...
>
> While China's methods in nearby waters bear some resemblance to *fin de siècle* America's, its goals could hardly be more different. The difference is between closed seas and skies ruled by a strong coastal state and freedom of the maritime commons....
>
> [The United States] never claimed ownership of the greater Caribbean, however much it coveted primacy there. There was no American counterpart to the nine-dashed line.
>
> Nor, despite occasional glances toward Cuba and other islands, did Washington regard these jewels of the Caribbean as rightful U.S. property. Nor did any significant school of foreign-policy thought regard southern waters as a seaward extension of the North American landmass. Still less did official policy consider the sea sovereign territory or "blue national soil," to borrow the ubiquitous Chinese phrase for the near seas.
>
> Instead, the Monroe Doctrine was a unilateral directive forbidding European empires to reconquer American republics that had won their independence. The doctrine was popular in Latin America for decades....
>
> Only in the 1910s did the Monroe Doctrine truly fall into disrepute in Latin America. That's when U.S. leaders took to using it abusively, as a pretext for diplomatic and military interventionism rather than a common defense of the Americas.
>
> Yet U.S. statesmen didn't cling hardheadedly to even this most cherished of foreign-policy doctrines. In the 1920s, Washington retracted the Theodore Roosevelt "Corollary" to the doctrine, which Presidents William Howard Taft and Woodrow Wilson invoked as a license for intervention in Caribbean nations' affairs. Presidents Herbert Hoover and Franklin

---

[42] Robert D. Kaplan, "China's Budding Ocean Empire," *The National Interest (http://nationalinterest.org)*, June 5, 2014.

Roosevelt subsequently ushered in the pan-American defense system that remains in place to this day.

In effect Hoover and FDR internationalized the Monroe Doctrine, enlisting fellow American states as co-guarantors of hemispheric security. Can you imagine Beijing walking back its nine-dashed line in similar fashion? One can hope—but don't hold your breath.

So let's not drink the Kool-Aid Beijing is peddling. When it disavows its claim to "indisputable sovereignty" over the South China Sea, reverses longstanding policy to favor freedom of the seas and skies, and, most importantly, wins buy-in from Asian neighbors, then I'll be glad to welcome comparisons [with what the United States wanted to accomplish in the Caribbean Sea and the Gulf of Mexico in the age of the Monroe Doctrine].[43]

Chinese Actions Since Late 2013 That Have Heightened Concerns

Following a confrontation in 2012 between Chinese and Philippine ships at Scarborough Shoal, China gained *de facto* control over access to the shoal. Subsequent Chinese actions for asserting and defending China's claims in the ECS and SCS that have heightened concerns among observers, particularly since late 2013, include the following:

- ongoing Chinese pressure against the Philippine presence at Second Thomas Shoal, a submerged shoal in the Spratly Islands;[44]

- frequent patrols by Chinese Coast Guard ships—some observers refer to them as harassment operations—at the Senkaku Islands;

- China's announcement on November 23, 2013, of an air defense identification zone (ADIZ) for the ECS that includes airspace over the Senkaku Islands;

- the previously mentioned December 5, 2013, incident in which a Chinese navy ship put itself in the path of the U.S. Navy cruiser *Cowpens*, forcing the *Cowpens* to change course to avoid a collision;

- the implementation on January 1, 2014, of fishing regulations administered by China's Hainan province applicable to waters constituting more than half of the SCS, and the reported enforcement of those regulations with actions that have included the apprehension of non-Chinese fishing boats;[45]

- land-reclamation activities, publicly reported starting in May 2014, at locations in the SCS occupied by China that observers view as a prelude to the construction of expanded Chinese facilities and fortifications at those locations;[46] and

[43] James R. Holmes, "The Nine-Dashed Line Isn't China's Monroe Doctrine," *The Diplomat (http://thediplomat.com)*, June 21, 2014.

[44] For a discussion of the situation at Second Thomas Shoal, see "A Game of Shark And Minnow," *New York Times Magazine* online news graphic accessed March 10, 2014, at http://www.nytimes.com/newsgraphics/2013/10/27/south-china-sea/. See also Ben Blanchard, "China Says [It] Expels Philippine [Vessels] from Disputed Shoal," *Reuters.com*, March 10, 2014; Oliver Teves (Associated Press), "Philippines Protests China Stopping Troop Resupply," *Kansas City Star (www.kansascity.com)*, March 11, 2014; Kyodo News International, "Philippines Protests Chinese Actions in Disputed Sea," *Global Post (www.globalpost.com)*, March 3, 2014.

[45] See, for example, Natalie Thomas, Ben Blanchard, and Megha Rajagopalan, "China Apprehending Boats Weekly in Disputed South China Sea," *Reuters.com*, March 6, 2014.

[46] See, for example, Edward Wong and Jonathan Ansfield, "To Bolster Its Claims, China Plants Islands in Disputed (continued...)

- moving a large oil rig in May 2014 into waters that are near the Paracels and inside Vietnam's claimed EEZ, and using dozens of Chinese Coast Guard and Chinese navy ships to enforce a large keep-away zone around the rig, leading to numerous confrontations and incidents between Chinese and Vietnamese civilian and military ships.[47]

At a February 5, 2014, hearing before the subcommittee on Asia and the Pacific of the House Foreign Affairs Committee, Assistant Secretary of State Daniel Russel testified that

> Deputy Secretary [of State William J.] Burns and I were in Beijing earlier this month to hold regular consultations with the Chinese government on Asia-Pacific issues, and we held extensive discussions regarding our concerns. These include continued restrictions on access to Scarborough Reef; pressure on the long-standing Philippine presence at the Second Thomas Shoal; putting hydrocarbon blocks up for bid in an area close to another country's mainland and far away even from the islands that China is claiming; announcing administrative and even military districts in contested areas in the South China Sea; an unprecedented spike in risky activity by China's maritime agencies near the Senkaku Islands; the sudden, uncoordinated and unilateral imposition of regulations over contested airspace in the case of the East China Sea Air Defense Identification Zone; and the recent updating of fishing regulations covering disputed areas in the South China Sea. These actions have raised tensions in the region and concerns about China's objectives in both the South China and the East China Seas.
>
> There is a growing concern that this pattern of behavior in the South China Sea reflects an incremental effort by China to assert control over the area contained in the so-called "nine-dash line," despite the objections of its neighbors and despite the lack of any explanation or apparent basis under international law regarding the scope of the claim itself.[48]

(...continued)

Waters," *New York Times (www.nytimes.com)*, June 16, 2014; Trefor Moss, "China Rejects Philippines' Call for Construction Freeze," *Wall Street Journal (http://online.wsj.com)*, June 16, 2014; Wendell Minnick, "Beijing Continues S. China Sea Expansion," *Defense News (www.defensenews.com)*, June 14, 2014; Joel Guinto, "China Building Dubai-Style Fake Islands in South China Sea," Bloomberg News (www.bloomberg.com), June 11, 2014; David Dizon, "Why China Military Base in West PH Sea Is A 'Game-Changer,'" ABS-CBN News (www.abs-cbnnews.com), June 10, 2014.

[47] One observer writes: "Since that unilateral maneuver [of the oil rig] in early May, China has created a *cordon sanitaire* around the rig by deploying military, coast guard, and fishing vessels in three concentric patrol circles. To date, a Vietnamese fishing vessel has been sunk and China has made unsubstantiated claims that Vietnamese boats have hit Chinese vessels on more than 1,400 occasions. Dueling videos are currently on the internet. While Vietnamese behavior is not beyond reproach, China might have a better case to make if it would adhere to international law. China has every right to protect a drilling rig inside its territorial waters, but a rig outside of its 12-nautical-mile territorial waters is entitled to only a 500-meter safety zone." (Patrick M. Cronin, "US Should Help Vietnam Counter China's Coercion," *Asia Pacific Bulletin (www.eastwestcenter.org)*, Number 269, June 26, 2014.)

[48] Testimony of Daniel Russel, Assistant Secretary of State, Bureau of East Asian and Pacific Affairs, U.S. Department of State, Before the House Committee on Foreign Affairs, Subcommittee on Asia and the Pacific, Wednesday, February 5, 2014, [on] Maritime Disputes in East Asia, pp. 5-6.

U.S. Position on These Issues

Some Key Elements

The U.S. position on territorial and EEZ disputes in the Western Pacific (including those involving China) includes the following elements, among others:

- The United States takes no position on competing claims to sovereignty over disputed land features in the ECS and SCS.

- Claims of territorial waters and EEZs should be consistent with customary international law of the sea and must therefore, among other things, derive from land features. Claims in the SCS that are not derived from land features are fundamentally flawed.

- Territorial disputes should be resolved peacefully, without coercion, intimidation, threats, or the use of force.

- Parties should avoid taking provocative or unilateral actions that disrupt the status quo or jeopardize peace and security; the Senkaku Islands are under the administration of Japan and unilateral attempts to change the status quo raise tensions and do nothing under international law to strengthen territorial claims.

- The United States has a national interest in the preservation of freedom of seas as recognized in customary international law of the sea. The United States opposes claims that impinge on the rights, freedoms, and lawful uses of the sea that belong to all nations.

- The United States, like most other countries, believes that coastal states under UNCLOS have the right to regulate economic activities in their EEZs, but do not have the right to regulate foreign military activities in their EEZs.

February 5, 2014, State Department Testimony

At a February 5, 2014, hearing before the subcommittee on Asia and the Pacific of the House Foreign Affairs Committee, Assistant Secretary of State Daniel Russel testified that

> Since the end of the Second World War, a maritime regime based on international law that promotes freedom of navigation and lawful uses of the sea has facilitated Asia's impressive economic growth. The United States, through our our [sic] alliances, our security partnerships and our overall military presence and posture, has been instrumental in sustaining that maritime regime and providing the security that has enabled the countries in the region to prosper. As a maritime nation with global trading networks, the United States has a national interest in freedom of the seas and in unimpeded lawful commerce. From President Thomas Jefferson's actions against the Barbary pirates to President Reagan's decision that the United States will abide by the Law of the Sea Convention's provisions on navigation and other traditional uses of the ocean, American foreign policy has long defended the freedom of the seas. And as we consistently state, we have a national interest in the maintenance of peace and stability; respect for international law; unimpeded lawful commerce; and freedom of navigation and overflight in the East China and South China Seas....

Mr. Chairman, we have a deep and long-standing stake in the maintenance of prosperity and stability in the Asia-Pacific and an equally deep and abiding long-term interest in the continuance of freedom of the seas based on the rule of law—one that guarantees, among other things, freedom of navigation and overflight and other internationally lawful uses of the sea related to those freedoms. International law makes clear the legal basis on which states can legitimately assert their rights in the maritime domain or exploit marine resources. By promoting order in the seas, international law is instrumental in safeguarding the rights and freedoms of all countries regardless of size or military strength.

I think it is imperative that we be clear about what we mean when the United States says that we take no position on competing claims to sovereignty over disputed land features in the East China and South China Seas. First of all, we do take a strong position with regard to behavior in connection with any claims: we firmly oppose the use of intimidation, coercion or force to assert a territorial claim. Second, we do take a strong position that maritime claims must accord with customary international law. This means that all maritime claims must be derived from land features and otherwise comport with the international law of the sea. So while we are not siding with one claimant against another, we certainly believe that claims in the South China Sea that are not derived from land features are fundamentally flawed. In support of these principles and in keeping with the longstanding U.S. Freedom of Navigation Program, the United States continues to oppose claims that impinge on the rights, freedoms, and lawful uses of the sea that belong to all nations.

As I just noted, we care deeply about the way countries behave in asserting their claims or managing their disputes. We seek to ensure that territorial and maritime disputes are dealt with peacefully, diplomatically and in accordance with international law. Of course this means making sure that shots aren't fired; but more broadly it means ensuring that these disputes are managed without intimidation, coercion, or force. We have repeatedly made clear that freedom of navigation is reflected in international law, not something to be granted by big states to others....

China's lack of clarity with regard to its South China Sea claims has created uncertainty, insecurity and instability in the region. It limits the prospect for achieving a mutually agreeable resolution or equitable joint development arrangements among the claimants. I want to reinforce the point that under international law, maritime claims in the South China Sea must be derived from land features. Any use of the "nine dash line" by China to claim maritime rights not based on claimed land features would be inconsistent with international law. The international community would welcome China to clarify or adjust its nine-dash line claim to bring it in accordance with the international law of the sea.

We support serious and sustained diplomacy between the claimants to address overlapping claims in a peaceful, non-coercive way. This can and should include bilateral as well as multilateral diplomatic dialogue among the claimants. But at the same time we fully support the right of claimants to exercise rights they may have to avail themselves of peaceful dispute settlement mechanisms. The Philippines chose to exercise such a right last year with the filing of an arbitration case under the Law of the Sea Convention.[49]

---

[49] Testimony of Daniel Russel, Assistant Secretary of State, Bureau of East Asian and Pacific Affairs, U.S. Department of State, Before the House Committee on Foreign Affairs, Subcommittee on Asia and the Pacific, Wednesday, February 5, 2014, [on] Maritime Disputes in East Asia, pp. 2, 4-5, 6.

May 31, 2014, Secretary of Defense Speech

On May 31, 2014, in a speech at an international conference in Singapore called the Shangri-La Dialogue, Secretary of Defense Chuck Hagel stated in part:

> One of the most critical tests facing the region is whether nations will choose to resolve disputes through diplomacy and well-established international rules and norms…or through intimidation and coercion. Nowhere is this more evident than in the South China Sea, the beating heart of the Asia-Pacific and a crossroads for the global economy.
>
> China has called the South China Sea "a sea of peace, friendship, and cooperation." And that's what it should be.
>
> But in recent months, China has undertaken destabilizing, unilateral actions asserting its claims in the South China Sea. It has restricted access to Scarborough Reef, put pressure on the long-standing Philippine presence at the Second Thomas Shoal, begun land reclamation activities at multiple locations, and moved an oil rig into disputed waters near the Paracel Islands.
>
> The United States has been clear and consistent. We take no position on competing territorial claims. But we firmly oppose any nation's use of intimidation, coercion, or the threat of force to assert those claims.
>
> We also oppose any effort—by any nation—to restrict overflight or freedom of navigation—whether from military or civilian vessels, from countries big or small. The United States will not look the other way when fundamental principles of the international order are being challenged.
>
> We will uphold those principles. We made clear last November that the U.S. military would not abide by China's unilateral declaration of an Air Defense Identification Zone in the East China Sea, including over the Japanese-administered Senkaku Islands. And as President Obama clearly stated in Japan last month, the Senkaku Islands are under the mutual defense treaty with Japan.
>
> All nations of the region, including China, have a choice: to unite, and recommit to a stable regional order, or to walk away from that commitment and risk the peace and security that have benefitted millions of people throughout the Asia-Pacific, and billions around the world.
>
> The United States will support efforts by any nation to lower tensions and peacefully resolve disputes in accordance with international law.
>
> We all know that cooperation is possible. Last month, 21 nations signed the Code for Unplanned Encounters at Sea—an important naval safety protocol. ASEAN and China are negotiating a Code of Conduct for the South China Sea—and the United States encourages its early conclusion. Nations of the region have also agreed to joint energy exploration; this month, the Philippines and Indonesia resolved a longstanding maritime boundary dispute; and this week, Taiwan and the Philippines agreed to sign a new fisheries agreement.
>
> China, too, has agreed to third-party dispute resolution in the World Trade Organization; peacefully resolved a maritime boundary dispute with Vietnam in 2000; and signed ASEAN's Treaty of Amity and Cooperation.

For all our nations, the choices are clear, and the stakes are high. These stakes are not just about the sovereignty of rocky shoals and island reefs, or even the natural resources that surround them and lie beneath them. They are about sustaining the Asia-Pacific's rules-based order, which has enabled the people of this region to strengthen their security, allowing for progress and prosperity. That is the order the United States—working with our partners and allies—that is the order that has helped underwrite since the end of World War II. And it is the order we will continue to support—around the world, and here in the Asia-Pacific.[50]

June 25, 2014, State Department Testimony

At a June 25, 2014, hearing before the Senate Foreign Relations Committee, Assistant Secretary of State Daniel Russel testified that

We believe all countries, and particularly emerging powers like China, should recognize the self-benefit of upholding basic rules and norms on which the international system is built; these are rules and norms which China has participated in formulating and shaping, and they are rules and norms that it continues to benefit from. In this context, we are encouraging China to exercise restraint in dealing with its neighbors and show respect for universal values and international law both at home and abroad....

In the Asia-Pacific region, Beijing's neighbors are understandably alarmed by China's increasingly coercive efforts to assert and enforce its claims in the South China and East China Seas. A pattern of unilateral Chinese actions in sensitive and disputed areas is raising tensions and damaging China's international standing. Moreover, some of China's actions are directed at U.S. treaty allies. The United States has important interests at stake in these seas: freedom of navigation and overflight, unimpeded lawful commerce, respect for international law, and the peaceful management of disputes. We apply the same principles to the behavior of all claimants involved, not only to China. China—as a strong and rising power—should hold itself to a high standard of behavior; to willfully disregard diplomatic and other peaceful ways of dealing with disagreements and disputes in favor of economic or physical coercion is destabilizing and dangerous.

The United States does not take sides on the sovereignty questions underlying the territorial disputes in the South and East China Seas, but we have an interest in the behavior of states in their management or resolution of these disputes. We want countries, including China, to manage or settle claims through peaceful, diplomatic means. For example, the Philippines and Indonesia have just done so in connection with their EEZ boundary. Disputes can also be addressed through third-party dispute resolution processes. Where parties' rights under treaties may be affected, some treaties provide for third-party dispute settlement, as is the case of the Law of the Sea Convention, an avenue pursued by the Philippines in an arbitration with China currently being considered by an Arbitral Tribunal constituted under that treaty. The United States and the international community oppose the use or the threat of force to try to advance a claim, and view such actions as having no effect in strengthening the legitimacy of China's claims. These issues should be decided on the basis of the merits of China's and other claimants' legal claims and adherence to international law and norms, not the strength of their militaries and law enforcement ships or the size of their economies.[51]

---

[50] Secretary of Defense Speech, IISS Shangri-La Dialogue, As Delivered by Secretary of Defense Chuck Hagel, May 31, 2014, accessed June 6, 2014, at http://www.defense.gov/Speeches/Speech.aspx?SpeechID=1857. Ellipse in the first paragraph as in the original.

[51] Testimony of Daniel Russel, Assistant Secretary of State, Bureau of East Asian and Pacific Affairs, U.S. Department of State, Before the Senate Foreign Relations Committee, [on] The Future of U.S.-China Relations, June 25, 2014, pp. (continued...)

Operational Rights in EEZs

Regarding a coastal state's rights within its EEZ, Scot Marciel, then-Deputy Assistant Secretary, Bureau of East Asian and Pacific Affairs, stated the following as part of his prepared statement for a July 15, 2009, hearing before the East Asian and Pacific Affairs subcommittee of the Senate Foreign Relations Committee:

> I would now like to discuss recent incidents involving China and the activities of U.S. vessels in international waters within that country's Exclusive Economic Zone (EEZ). In March 2009, the survey ship USNS Impeccable was conducting routine operations, consistent with international law, in international waters in the South China Sea. Actions taken by Chinese fishing vessels to harass the Impeccable put ships of both sides at risk, interfered with freedom of navigation, and were inconsistent with the obligation for ships at sea to show due regard for the safety of other ships. We immediately protested those actions to the Chinese government, and urged that our differences be resolved through established mechanisms for dialogue—not through ship-to-ship confrontations that put sailors and vessels at risk.
>
> Our concern over that incident centered on China's conception of its legal authority over other countries' vessels operating in its Exclusive Economic Zone (EEZ) and the unsafe way China sought to assert what it considers its maritime rights.
>
> China's view of its rights on this specific point is not supported by international law. We have made that point clearly in discussions with the Chinese and underscored that U.S. vessels will continue to operate lawfully in international waters as they have done in the past.[52]

As part of his prepared statement for the same hearing, Robert Scher, then-Deputy Assistant Secretary of Defense, Asian and Pacific Security Affairs, Office of the Secretary of Defense, stated that

> we reject any nation's attempt to place limits on the exercise of high seas freedoms within an exclusive economic zones [sic] (EEZ). Customary international law, as reflected in articles 58 and 87 of the 1982 United Nations Convention on the Law of the Sea, guarantees to all nations the right to exercise within the EEZ, high seas freedoms of navigation and overflight, as well as the traditional uses of the ocean related to those freedoms. It has been the position of the United States since 1982 when the Convention was established, that the navigational rights and freedoms applicable within the EEZ are qualitatively and quantitatively the same as those rights and freedoms applicable on the high seas. We note that almost 40% of the world's oceans lie within the 200 nautical miles EEZs, and it is essential to the global economy and international peace and security that navigational rights and freedoms within the EEZ be vigorously asserted and preserved.
>
> As previously noted, our military activity in this region is routine and in accordance with customary international law as reflected in the 1982 Law of the Sea Convention.[53]

(...continued)

2, 7-8.

[52] [Statement of] Deputy Assistant Secretary Scot Marciel, Bureau of East Asian & Pacific Affairs, U.S. Department of State, before the Subcommittee on East Asian and Pacific Affairs, Committee on Foreign Relations, United States Senate, July 15, 2009, [hearing on] Maritime Issues and Sovereignty Disputes in East Asia, p. 5.

[53] Testimony [prepared statement] of Deputy Assistant Secretary of Defense Robert Scher, Asian and Pacific Security (continued...)

U.S. Freedom of Navigation (FON) Program

U.S. Navy ships carry out assertions of operational rights as part of the U.S. Freedom of Navigation (FON) program for challenging maritime claims that the United States believes to be inconsistent with international law.[54] The Department of Defense's (DOD's) record of "excessive maritime claims that were challenged by DoD operational assertions and activities during the period of October 1, 2012, to September 30, 2013, in order to preserve the rights, freedoms, and uses of the sea and airspace guaranteed to all nations in international law" includes a listing for multiple challenges that were conducted to challenge Chinese claims relating to "excessive straight baselines; security jurisdiction in contiguous zone; jurisdiction over airspace above the exclusive economic zone (EEZ); domestic law criminalizing survey activity by foreign entities in EEZ; [and] prior permission required for innocent passage of foreign military ships through territorial sea."[55]

Potential Implications for United States

China's actions for asserting and defending its maritime territorial and EEZ claims in the ECS and SCS, particularly since late 2013, have heightened concerns among observers that ongoing disputes over these waters and some of the islands within them could lead to a crisis or conflict between China and a neighboring country such as Japan, the Philippines, or Vietnam, and that the United States could be drawn into such a crisis or conflict as a result of obligations the United States has under bilateral security treaties with Japan and the Philippines.

(...continued)

Affairs, Office of the Secretary of Defense, before the Subcommittee on East Asian and Pacific Affairs, Senate Committee on Foreign Relations, United States Senate, July 15, 2009, [hearing on] Maritime Issues and Sovereignty Disputes in East Asia, pp. 3-4. See also Raul (Pete) Pedrozo, "Preserving Navigational Rights and Freedoms: The Right to Conduct Military Activities in China's Exclusive Economic Zone," *Chinese Journal of International Law*, 2010: 9-29.

[54] The State Department states that

> U.S. Naval forces engage in Freedom of Navigation operations to assert the principles of International Law and free passage in regions with unlawful maritime sovereignty claims. FON operations involve naval units transiting disputed areas to avoid setting the precedent that the international community has accepted these unlawful claims. ISO coordinates DOS clearance for FON operations.
>
> (Source: State Department website on military operational issues, accessed March 22, 2013, at http://www.state.gov/t/pm/iso/c21539 htm. See also the web page posted at http://www.state.gov/e/oes/ocns/opa/maritimesecurity/index.htm.)

A DOD list of DOD Instructions (available at http://www.dtic mil/whs/directives/corres/ins1 html) includes a listing for DOD Instruction C-2005.01 of October 12, 2005, on the FON program, and states that this instruction replaced an earlier version of the document dated June 21, 1983. The document itself is controlled and not posted at the website. A website maintained by the Federation of American Scientists (FAS) listing Presidential Decision Directives (PDDs) of the Clinton Administration for the years 1993-2000 (http://www fas.org/irp/offdocs/pdd/index html) states that PDD-32 concerned the FON program. The listing suggests that PDD-32 was issued between September 21, 1994 and February 17, 1995.

[55] U.S. Department of Defense (DOD) Freedom of Navigation (FON) Report for Fiscal Year (FY) 2013, accessed March 10, 2014, at http://policy.defense.gov/Portals/11/Documents/gsa/cwmd/FY2013%20DOD%20Annual%20FON%20Report.pdf. Similar reports for prior fiscal years are posted at http://policy.defense.gov/OUSDPOffices/FON.aspx.

More broadly, China's actions for asserting and defending its maritime territorial and EEZ claims have led to increasing concerns among some observers that China may be seeking to dominate or gain control of its near-seas region, meaning the ECS, the SCS, and the Yellow Sea.[56] Chinese domination over or control of this region could have major implications for the United States, including implications for U.S.-China relations, for interpreting China's rise as a major world power, for the security structure of the Asia-Pacific region, for the long-standing U.S. strategic goal of preventing the emergence of a regional hegemon in one part of Eurasia or another, and for two key elements of the U.S.-led international order that has operated since World War II—the non-use of force or coercion as a means of settling disputes between countries, and freedom of the seas.

---

[56] For example, one observer states that "The long and ongoing record of unilateral Chinese assertions or aggressions in the South and East China Sea no longer leaves room for doubt as to Beijing's intention. China wants and is trying to achieve dominance over the waters behind what it calls the 'first island chain' and land features that fringe the U-shaped line. The question is not 'what does China intend?' The answer—dominance of some kind and degree—is known. The question is 'what, if anything, is anyone else prepared to do?'" (Donald K. Emmerson, "China Challenges Philippines in the South China Sea," *East Asia Forum* (*www.eastasiaforum.org*), March 18, 2014.)

Another observer states that "For more than a decade, the Chinese government has been pursuing a deliberate, yet indirect strategy to establish de facto control over the waters and airspace adjacent to its mainland." (Daniel Goure, "New Chinese Air Defense Zone Is latest Move In Beijing's Strategy To Dominate East Asia," Lexington Institute Early Warnnig Blog (www.lexingtoninstitute.org), November 25, 2013.) A December 4, 2013, press report states: "China's escalation in its challenge to Japan's administration of islands near Taiwan reflects an effort to gain greater command of the air and seas in the western Pacific as it builds itself into a maritime power." (Henry Sanderson and Shai Oster, "China Air Zone Seen Step to Expanding Access to West Pacific," *Bloomberg News* (*www.bloomberg.com*), December 4, 2013.

Another observer states that "Beijing seeks to wield this growing might to pursue outstanding territorial and maritime claims and to carve out in the Yellow, East and South China Seas and airspace above them a 'zone of exceptionalism' within which existing global security, legal, and resource management norms are subordinated to its parochial national interests. This can only weaken the global system on which all nations' security and prosperity depends, and will continue to destabilize a vital but vulnerable region that remains haunted by history." (Andrew S. Erickson, "Deterrence by Denial: How to Prevent China From Using Force," National Interest (http://nationalinterest.org), December 16, 2013.)

Another observer states that "The Chinese have long felt vulnerable from the sea and their current maritime strategy seeks to reduce that vulnerability by extending a ring of maritime control around China's periphery.... *First and foremost, it is the failure of previous Chinese leaders to close the maritime gap in China's arc of security and the invasions that resulted that motivates China's current leaders to extend strategic power over the near seas. Extending Chinese control over the near seas therefore is seen as enhancing security for the Chinese state and healing a sort of psychological wound in the collective Chinese mind.*" (Statement of Peter A. Dutton, Professor and Director, China Maritime Studies Institute, U.S. Naval War College, Testimony before the House Foreign Affairs Committee Hearing on China's Maritime Disputes in the East and South China Seas, January 14, 2014, pp. 2, 3. Italics as in original. [The hearing was actually a joint hearing before Seapower and Projection Forces subcommittee of the House Armed Services Committee and the Asia and the Pacific subcommittee of the House Foreign Affairs Committee.])

Another observer states that "The Yalong Bay naval base on [China's] Hainan [island] is one part of the strategy that China is starting to put in place to exert control over the Near Seas, pushing the US Navy ever farther out into the Western Pacific.... By weakening the US naval presence in the western Pacific, China hopes gradually to undermine America's alliances with other Asian countries, notably South Korea, the Philippines and maybe even Japan. If US influence declines, China would be in a position to assume quietly a leadership position in Asia, giving it much greater sway over the rules and practices in the global economy.... China's stepped-up claim over the [Senkaku] islands is one art of its push for greater control of the surrounding seas but it is also a central part of the growing contest for influence with the US." (Geoff Dyer, "US v China: Is This The New Cold War?" *Financial Times* (*www.ft.com*), February 20, 2014.

Another observer states that China's ECS ADIZ "can be regarded as just one element in a larger strategy of trying to assert sovereignty in the East China Sea and vast parts of the South China Sea, as reflected in Beijing's 'nine-dashed line.'" (Benjamin Schreer, "China's Rise: The Strategic Climate Is Getting Colder," *The Strategist (The Australian Strategic Policy Institute Blog)*, March 3, 2014.

Risk of United States Being Drawn Into a Crisis or Conflict

Many observers are concerned that ongoing maritime territorial disputes in the ECS and SCS could lead to a crisis or conflict between China and a neighboring country such as Japan, the Philippines, and that the United States could be drawn into such a crisis or conflict as a result of obligations the United States has under bilateral security treaties with Japan and the Philippines. U.S. officials, concerned about the risk that a misunderstanding or miscalculation might cause a dispute over island territories to escalate into a conflict, have urged parties involved in the disputes to exercise restraint and avoid taking provocative actions.

U.S.-Japan Treaty on Mutual Cooperation and Security

The 1960 U.S.-Japan treaty on mutual cooperation and security[57] states in Article V that

> Each Party recognizes that an armed attack against either Party in the territories under the administration of Japan would be dangerous to its own peace and safety and declares that it would act to meet the common danger in accordance with its constitutional provisions and processes.

The United States has reaffirmed on a number of occasions over the years that since the Senkaku Islands are under the administration of Japan, they are included in the territories referred to in Article V of the treaty, and that the United States "will honor all of our treaty commitments to our treaty partners."[58] (At the same time, the United States, noting the difference between administration and sovereignty, has noted that such affirmations do not prejudice the U.S. approach of taking no position regarding the outcome of the dispute between China, Taiwan, and Japan regarding who has sovereignty over the islands.) Some observers, while acknowledging the U.S. affirmations, have raised questions regarding the potential scope of actions that the United States might take under Article V.[59]

---

[57] Treaty of mutual cooperation and security, signed January 19, 1960, entered into force June 23, 1960, 11 UST 1632; TIAS 4509; 373 UNTS.

[58] The quoted words are from Secretary of Defense Chuck Hagel, in "Media Availability with Secretary Hagel En Route to Japan," April 5, 2014, accessed April 9, 2014, at http://www.defense.gov/transcripts/transcript.aspx?transcriptid=5405. See also Associated Press, "US: Will Stand by Allies in Disputes with China," *Military.com*, April 3, 2014.

[59] See, for example, Yoichiro Sato, "The Senkaku Dispute and the US-Japan Security Treaty," PacNet #57 (Pacific Forum CSIS, Honolulu, Hawaii), September 10, 2012, accessed October 2, 2012, at http://csis.org/files/publication/Pac1257.pdf; James R. Holmes, "Thucydides, Japan and America," *The Diplomat* (http://thediplomat.com/the-naval-diplomat), November 27, 2012; Shigemi Sato, "Japan, U.S. To Discuss Revising Defense Guidelines," *DefenseNews.com* (*Agence France-Presse*), November 11, 2012; Martin Fackler, "Japan Seeks Tighter Pact With U.S. To Confront China," *NYTimes.com*, November 9, 2012; "Japan, U.S. To Review Defense Guidelines," *Japan Times*, November 11, 2012; "Defense Official To Visit U.S. To Discuss Alliance," *Kyodo News*, November 8, 2012; Yuka Hayashi, "U.S. Commander Chides China Over 'Provocative Act,'" *Wall Street Journal*, February 16, 2013: 7; Julian E. Barnes, "U.S., Japan Update Plans To Defend Islands," *New York Times*, March 20, 2013. See also Kiyoshi Takenaka, "China "Extremely Concerned" About U.S.-Japan Island Talk, *Reuters* (http://in reuters.com), March 21, 2013; Wendell, Minnick, "Senkakus Could Be Undoing of Asia Pivot," *Defense News*, April 15, 2013: 16; Item entitled "U.S. Warns China" in Bill Gertz, "Inside the Ring: NSA Contractor Threat," Washington Times, June 19, 2013; Anthony Fensom, "Yamaguchi: China Military Build-Up Risks Accident," *The Diplomat* (http://thediplomat.com), June 21, 2013.

U.S.-Philippines Mutual Defense Treaty[60]

The 1951 U.S.-Philippines mutual defense treaty[61] states in Article IV that

> Each Party recognizes that an armed attack in the Pacific Area on either of the Parties would be dangerous to its own peace and safety and declares that it would act to meet the common dangers in accordance with its constitutional processes.

Article V states that

> For the purpose of Article IV, an armed attack on either of the Parties is deemed to include an armed attack on the metropolitan territory of either of the Parties, or on the island territories under its jurisdiction in the Pacific or on its armed forces, public vessels or aircraft in the Pacific.

The United States has reaffirmed on a number of occasions over the years its obligations under the U.S.-Philippines mutual defense treaty.[62] On May 9, 2012, Filipino Foreign Affairs Secretary Albert F. del Rosario issued a statement providing the Philippine perspective regarding the treaty's application to territorial disputes in the SCS.[63] U.S. officials have made their own statements regarding the treaty's application to territorial disputes in the SCS.[64]

U.S.-China Relations

Developments regarding China's maritime territorial and EEZ disputes in the ECS and SCS could affect U.S.-China relations in general, which could have implications for other issues in U.S.-China relations.[65]

Interpreting China's Rise as a Major World Power

As China emerges as a major world power, observers are assessing what kind of international actor China will be. China's actions in asserting and defending its maritime territorial and EEZ disputes in the ECS and SCS could influence assessments that observers might make on issues such as China's approach to settling disputes between states (including whether China views

---

[60] For additional discussion of U.S. obligations under the U.S.-Philippines mutual defense treaty, see CRS Report RL33233, *The Republic of the Philippines and U.S. Interests*, by Thomas Lum.

[61] Mutual defense treaty, signed August 30, 1951, entered into force August 27, 1952, 3 UST 3947, TIAS 2529, 177 UNTS 133.

[62] See, for example, the Joint Statement of the United States-Philippines Ministerial Dialogue of April 30, 2012, available at http://www.state.gov/r/pa/prs/ps/2012/04/188977 htm, which states in part that "The United States and the Republic of the Philippines reaffirm our shared obligations under the Mutual Defense Treaty, which remains the foundation of the U.S.-Philippines security relationship." See also Associated Press, "US: Will Stand by Allies in Disputes with China," *Military.com*, April 3, 2014.

[63] Statement of Secretary del Rosario regarding the Philippines-U.S. Mutual Defense Treaty, May 9, 2012, accessed September 20, 2012, at http://www.gov.ph/2012/05/09/statement-of-secretary-del-rosario-regarding-the-philippines-u-s-mutual-defense-treaty-may-9-2012/.

[64] See, for example, Agence France-Presse, "Navy Chief: US Would 'Help' Philippines In South China Sea," *DefenseNews.com*, February 13, 2014; Manuel Mogato, "U.S. Admiral Assures Philippines of Help in Disputed Sea," *Reuters.com*, February 13, 2014.

[65] For a survey of issues in U.S.-China relations, see CRS Report R41108, *U.S.-China Relations: An Overview of Policy Issues*, by Susan V. Lawrence.

---

force and coercion as acceptable means for settling such disputes, and consequently whether China believes that "might makes right"), China's views toward the meaning and application of international law, and whether China views itself more as a stakeholder and defender of the current international order, or alternatively, more as a revisionist power that will seek to change elements of that order that it does not like.

Security Structure of Asia-Pacific Region

Chinese domination over or control of its near-seas region could have significant implications for the security structure of the Asia-Pacific region. In particular, Chinese domination over or control of its near-seas area could greatly complicate the ability of the United States to fulfill its obligations to Taiwan under the Taiwan Relations Act (H.R. 2479/P.L. 96-8 of April 10, 1979).[66] It could also complicate the ability of the United States to fulfill its obligations under security and defense treaties with other countries in the region, particularly Japan, South Korea, the Philippines, and Thailand.[67] More generally, it could complicate the ability of the United States to operate U.S. forces in the Western Pacific for various purposes, including maintaining regional stability, conducting engagement and partnership-building operations, responding to crises, and executing war plans. Developments such as these could in turn encourage countries in the region to reexamine their own defense programs and foreign policies, potentially leading to a further change in the region's security structure.

U.S. Strategic Goal of Preventing Emergence of Regional Hegemon in Eurasia

Observers who are concerned that China may be seeking to dominate or gain control of its near-seas region in some cases go further, expressing concern that this may be part of a larger Chinese effort to become the hegemonic power in its region.[68] From a standpoint of U.S. strategic policy,

---

[66] For more on the Taiwan Relations Act, see CRS Report R41952, *U.S.-Taiwan Relationship: Overview of Policy Issues*, by Shirley A. Kan and Wayne M. Morrison.

[67] The United States has bilateral treaties with Japan, South Korea, and the Philippines. The United States and Thailand are parties to a Southeast Asia collective defense treaty that also includes the United Kingdom France, Australia, and New Zealand. The United States also has a separate treaty with Australia and New Zealand. For a summary of U.S. collective defense treaties, see the list posted at http://www.state.gov/s/l/treaty/collectivedefense/.

[68] One observer, for example, states that "Our approach has been, and must continue to be, that no one country dominates Asia. That objective, our role, and our strategic interests are being challenged by China. It is apparent in the growth in capability and capacity of the PLA (especially naval and air forces) and in the way China is defining (or redefining) maritime and air boundaries. Strategic space is being reshaped spatially by military capabilities and behaviorally by dubious maritime and airspace claims. The latter is particularly critical and points to a fundamental difference in our strategic competition with China." (Gary Roughead, "China, Time and Rebalancing," Hoover Institution (www.hoover.org), undated (but with copyright of 2014), accessed March 25, 2014, at http://www.hoover.org/taskforces/military-history/strategika/11/roughead.) Another observer states that "China has historically been the Middle Kingdom, and it is now reasserting its perceived right to hegemonic status in East Asia." (Jim Talent, "The Equilibrium of East Asia," *National Review Online* (http://www.nationalreview.com), December 5, 2013.) Another observer states that "it is not clear yet if indeed China seeks regional hegemony. But there is a growing consensus among American and Japanese analysts that this is indeed the case. By Chinese hegemony in Asia we broadly mean something akin to the United States' position in Latin America. We do not mean actual conquest. Almost no one believes China intends to annex even its weakest neighbors like Cambodia or North Korea. Rather, analysts expect a zone of super-ordinate influence over neighbors." (Robert E. Kelly, "What Would Chinese Hegemony Look Like?" *The Diplomat* (http://thediplomat.com), February 10, 2014.)

---

such an effort would be highly significant, because it has been a long-standing U.S. strategic goal to prevent the emergence of a regional hegemon in one part of Eurasia or another.[69]

Non-use of Force or Coercion as a Means of Settling Disputes Between Countries

A key element of the U.S.-led international order that has operated since World War II is that force or coercion should not be used as a means of settling disputes between countries, and certainly not as a routine or first-resort method. Some observers are concerned that some of China's actions in asserting and defending its territorial claims in the ECS and SCS challenge this principal and help reestablish the very different principal of "might makes right" as a routine or defining characteristic of international relations.[70]

---

[69] Most of the world's people, resources, and economic activity are located not in the Western Hemisphere, but in the other hemisphere, particularly Eurasia. In response to this basic feature of world geography, U.S. policy makers for the last several decades have chosen to pursue, as a key element of U.S. national strategy, a goal of preventing the emergence of a regional hegemon in one part of Eurasia or another, on the grounds that such a hegemon could challenge core U.S. interests by, for example, denying the United States access to important resources and economic activity in part of Eurasia or establishing alliances with countries in the Western Hemisphere. Although U.S. policy makers do not often state this key national strategic goal explicitly in public, U.S. military operations in recent decades—both wartime operations and day-to-day operations—have been carried out in no small part in support of this key goal. One observer, for example, states that

> if a distant great power were to dominate Asia or Europe the way America dominates the Western Hemisphere, it would then be free to roam around the globe and form alliances with countries in the Wesern Hemisphere that have an adversarial relationship with the United States. In that circumstance, the stopping power of the Atlantic and Pacific oceans would be far less effective. Thus, American policy makers have a deep-seated interest in preventing another great power from achieving regional hegemony in Asia or Europe.

> The Persian Gulf is strategically important because it produces roughly 30 percent of the world's oil, and it holds about 55 percent of the world's cruide-oil reserves. If the flow of oil from that region were stopped or even severely curtailed for a substantial period of time, it would have a devastating effect on the world economy. Therefore, the United States has good reason to ensure that oil flows freely out of the Gulf, which in practice means preventing any single country from controlling all of that critical resource. Most oil-producing stattes will keep pumping and seeling their oil as long as they are free to do so, because they depend on the revenues. It is in America's interest to keep them that way, which means there can be no regional hegemon in the Gulf, as well as Asia and Europe....

> [The United States] should make sure it remains the most powerful country on the planet, which means making sure a rising China does not dominate Asia the way the United States dominates the Western Hemisphere.

> (John J. Mearsheimer, "America Unhinged," *National Interest* (http://nationalinterest.org), January 2, 2014. See also Robert Kagan, "Superpowers Don't Get to Retire," *New Republic (www.newrepublic.com)*, May 26, 2014.

[70] A "senior State Department official," in a background briefing, stated that "there is violent or strong agreement between the U.S. and ASEAN on the principles at stake, principles of freedom of navigation, principles of peaceful resolution. And those principles are, in fact, enshrined in the six points that ASEAN countries themselves have promulgated as guideposts for handling of the challenges of the South China Sea." (Department of State, Background Briefing En Route Brunei, October 9, 2013, accessed March 14, 2013, at http://www.state.gov/r/pa/prs/ps/2013/10/215222 htm.)

In a December 5, 2013, letter to China's Ambassor to the United States, Senators Robert Menendez, Bob Corker, Marco Rubio, and Benjamin L. Cardin stated:

> We view this unilateral action [by China to establish an ECS ADIZ] as an ill-conceived attempt to alter the status quo, increasing the possibility of misunderstanding or miscalculation. Moreover,

(continued...)

Freedom of the Seas

Another key element of the U.S.-led international order that has operated since World War II is the treatment of the world's seas under international law as international waters (i.e., as a global commons), and freedom of operations in international waters. The principal is often referred in shorthand as freedom of the seas. It is also sometimes referred to as freedom of navigation, although this term can be defined—particularly by parties who might not support freedom of the seas—in a narrow fashion, to include merely the freedom to navigate (i.e., pass through) sea areas, as opposed to the freedom for conducting various activities at sea. A more complete way to refer to the principal, as stated in DOD's annual FON report, is "the rights, freedoms, and uses of the sea and airspace guaranteed to all nations in international law."[71] The principal that most of the world's seas are to be treated under international law as international waters dates back hundreds of years.[72]

Some observers are concerned that China's maritime territorial claims, particularly as shown in the map of the nine-dash line, appear to challenge to the principal that the world's seas are to be treated under international law as international waters. If such a challenge were to gain acceptance in the SCS region, it would have broad implications for the United States and other countries not only in the SCS, but around the world, because international law is universal in application, and a challenge to a principal of international law in one part of the world, if accepted, can serve as a precedent for challenging it in other parts of the world. Overturning the principal of freedom of the seas, so that significant portions of the seas could be appropriated as

---

(...continued)

> this declaration reinforces the perception that China perfers coercion over rule of law mechanisms to address territorial, sovereignty or jurisdictional issues in the Asia-Pacific. It also follows a disturbing trend of increasingly hostile Chinese maritime activities, including repeated incursions by Chinese vessels into the waters and airspace of Japan, the Philippines, Vietnam and other in the East and South China Seas. These actions threaten freedom of air and maritime navigation, which are vital national interests of the United States."

Another observer states:

> Allowing Beijing to use force, or even the threat of force, to alter the regional status quo would have a number of pernicious effects. It would undermine the functioning of the most vibrant portion of the global commons—sea and air mediums that all nations rely on for trade and prosperity, but that none own. It would undermine important international norms and encourage the application of force to more of the world's many persistent disputes. Finally, it would threaten to destabilize a region haunted by history that has prospered during nearly seven decades of U.S. forces helping to preserve peace. No other nation has the capability and lack of territorial claims necessary to play this still-vital role.

> (Andrew S. Erickson, "China's Near-Seas Challenges," *National Review Online* (http://nationalinterest.org), January 13, 2014.

See also Jack David, "The Law of the Jungle Returns," *National Review Online*, March 6, 2014.

[71] U.S. Department of Defense (DOD) Freedom of Navigation (FON) Report for Fiscal Year (FY) 2013, accessed March 10, 2014, at http://policy.defense.gov/Portals/11/Documents/gsa/cwmd/ FY2013%20DOD%20Annual%20FON%20Report.pdf. Similar reports for prior fiscal years are posted at http://policy.defense.gov/OUSDPOffices/FON.aspx.

[72] The idea that most of the world's seas should be treated as international waters rather than as a space that could be appropriated as national territory dates back to Hugo Grotius (1583-1645), a founder of international law, whose 1609 book *Mare Liberum* ("The Free Sea") helped to establish the primacy of the idea over the competing idea, put forth by the legal jurist and scholar John Seldon (1584-1654) in his book 1635 book *Mare Clausum* ("Closed Sea"), that the sea could be appropriated as national territory, like the land.

---

national territory, would overthrow hundreds of years of international legal tradition relating to the legal status of the world's oceans.[73]

More specifically, if China's position on whether coastal states have a right under UNCLOS to regulate the activities of foreign military forces in their EEZs were to gain greater international acceptance under international law, it could substantially affect U.S. naval operations not only in the SCS and ECS (see **Figure 5** for EEZs in the SCS and ECS), but around the world, which in turn could substantially affect the ability of the United States to use its military forces to defend various U.S. interests overseas. As shown in **Figure 6**, significant portions of the world's oceans are claimable as EEZs, including high-priority U.S. Navy operating areas in the Western Pacific, the Persian Gulf, and the Mediterranean Sea.[74] The legal right of U.S. naval forces to operate freely in EEZ waters is important to their ability to perform many of their missions around the world, because many of those missions are aimed at influencing events ashore, and having to conduct operations from more than 200 miles offshore would reduce the inland reach and responsiveness of ship-based sensors, aircraft, and missiles, and make it more difficult to transport Marines and their equipment from ship to shore. Restrictions on the ability of U.S. naval forces to operate in EEZ waters could potentially require a change in U.S. military strategy or U.S. foreign policy goals.[75]

---

[73] One observer states:

> A very old debate has been renewed in recent years: is the sea a commons open to the free use of all seafaring states, or is it territory subject to the sovereignty of coastal states? Is it to be freedom of the seas, as Dutch jurist Hugo Grotius insisted? Or is it to be closed seas where strong coastal states make the rules, as Grotius' English archnemesis John Selden proposed?
>
> Customary and treaty law of the sea sides with Grotius, whereas China has in effect become a partisan of Selden. Just as England claimed dominion over the approaches to the British Isles, China wants to make the rules governing the China seas. Whose view prevails will determine not just who controls waters, islands, and atolls, but also the nature of the system of maritime trade and commerce. What happens in Asia could set a precedent that ripples out across the globe. The outcome of this debate is a big deal.
>
> (James R. Holmes, "Has China Awoken a Sleeping Giant in Japan?" *The Diplomat* (http://thediplomat.com), March 1, 2014.)

[74] The National Oceanic and Atmospheric Adminsitrartion (NOAA) calculates that EEZs account for about 30.4% of the world's oceans. (See the table called "Comparative Sizes of the Various Maritime Zones" at the end of "Maritime Zones and Boundaries, accessed Jun 6, 2014, at http://www.gc noaa.gov/gcil_maritime html, which states that EEZs account for 101.9 million square kilometers of the world's approximately 335.0 million square kilometers of oceans.

[75] See, for example, United States Senate, Committee on Foreign Relations, Committee on Foreign Relations, Hearing on Maritime Disputes and Sovereignty Issues in East Asia, July 15, 2009, Testimony of Peter Dutton, Associate Professor, China Maritime Studies Institute, U.S. Naval War College, pp. 2 and 6-7.

Figure 5. EEZs in South China Sea and East China Sea

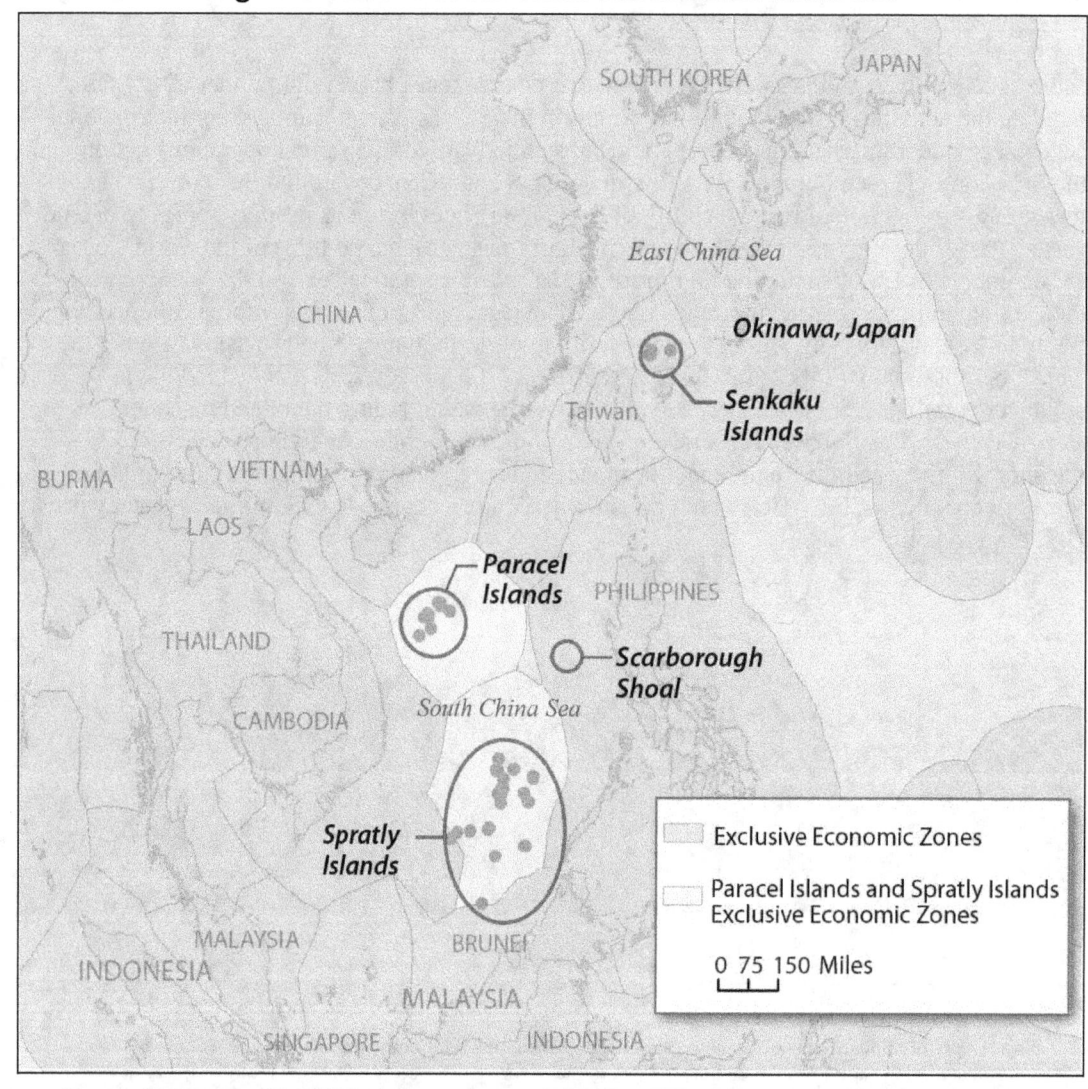

Source: Map prepared by CRS using basemaps provided by Esri. EEZs are from the Flanders Marine Institute (VLIZ) (2011). Maritime Boundaries Geodatabase, version 6. Available at http://www.vliz.be/vmdcdata/marbound.

Note: Disputed islands have been enlarged to make them more visible.

Figure 6. Claimable World EEZs

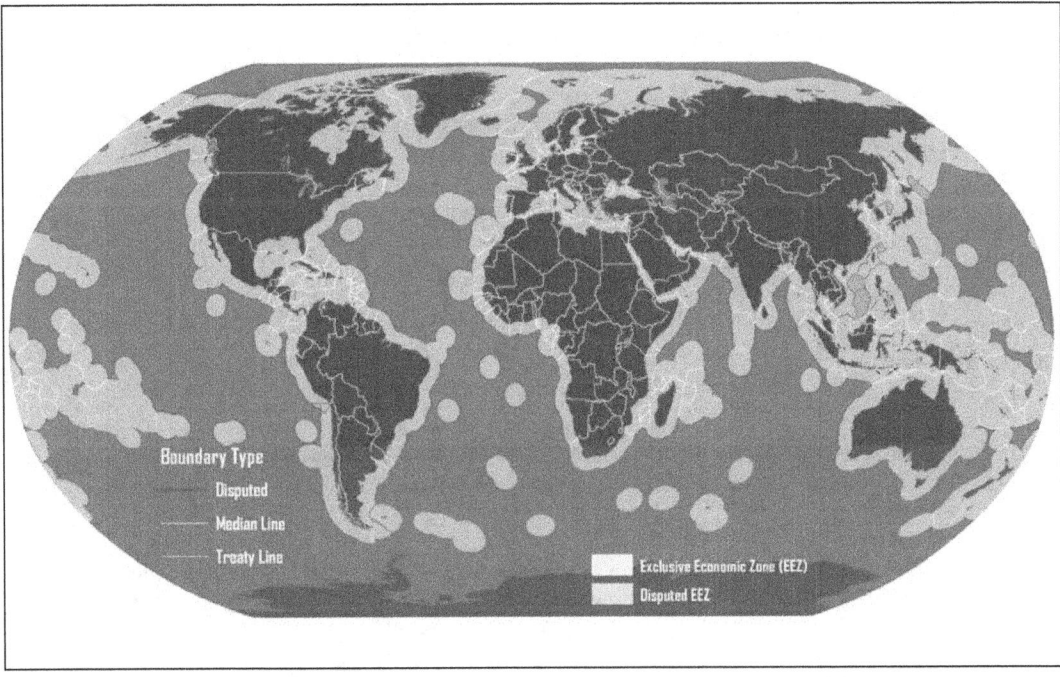

Source: Map designed by Dr. Jean-Paul Rodrigue, Department of Global Studies & Geography, Hofstra University, using boundaries plotted from Maritime Boundaries Geodatabase available at http://www.vliz.be/vmdcdata/marbound. The map is copyrighted and used here with permission. A version of the map is available at http://people.hofstra.edu/geotrans/eng/ch5en/conc5en/EEZ.html.

Some observers, in commenting on China's resistance to U.S. military survey and surveillance operations in China's EEZ, have argued that the United States would similarly dislike it if China or some other country were to conduct military survey or surveillance operations within the U.S. EEZ. Skeptics of this view might argue that U.S. policy accepts the right of other countries to operate their military forces freely in waters outside the 12-mile U.S. territorial waters limit, and that the United States during the Cold War acted in accordance with this position by not interfering with either Soviet ships (including intelligence-gathering vessels known as AGIs)[76] that operated close to the United States or with Soviet bombers and surveillance aircraft that periodically flew close to U.S. airspace. The U.S. Navy states that

---

[76] AGI was a U.S. Navy classification for the Soviet vessels in question in which the A meant auxiliary ship, the G meant miscellaneous purpose, and the I meant that the miscellaneous purpose was intelligence gathering. One observer states:

> During the Cold War it was hard for an American task force of any consequence to leave port without a Soviet "AGI" in trail. These souped-up fishing trawlers would shadow U.S. task forces, joining up just outside U.S. territorial waters. So ubiquitous were they that naval officers joked about assigning the AGI a station in the formation, letting it follow along—as it would anyway—without obstructing fleet operations.

> AGIs were configured not just to cast nets, but to track ship movements, gather electronic intelligence, and observe the tactics, techniques, and procedures by which American fleets transact business in great waters.

> (James R. Holmes, "China's Small Stick Diplomacy," *The Diplomat* (http://thediplomat.com), May 21, 2012, accessed October 3, 2012, at http://thediplomat.com/2012/05/21/chinas-small-stick-diplomacy/)

When the commonly recognized outer limit of the territorial sea under international law was three nautical miles, the United States recognized the right of other states, including the Soviet Union, to exercise high seas freedoms, including surveillance and other military operations, beyond that limit. The 1982 Law of the Sea Convention moved the outer limit of the territorial sea to twelve nautical miles. In 1983, President Reagan declared that the United States would accept the balance of the interests relating to the traditional uses of the oceans reflected in the 1982 Convention and would act in accordance with those provisions in exercising its navigational and overflight rights as long as other states did likewise. He further proclaimed that all nations will continue to enjoy the high seas rights and freedoms that are not resource related, including the freedoms of navigation and overflight, in the Exclusive Economic Zone he established for the United States consistent with the 1982 Convention.[77]

DOD states that

> the PLA Navy has begun to conduct military activities within the Exclusive Economic Zones (EEZs) of other nations, without the permission of those coastal states. Of note, the United States has observed over the past year several instances of Chinese naval activities in the EEZ around Guam and Hawaii. One of those instances was during the execution of the annual Rim of the Pacific (RIMPAC) exercise in July/August 2012. While the United States considers the PLA Navy activities in its EEZ to be lawful, the activity undercuts China's decades-old position that similar foreign military activities in China's EEZ are unlawful.[78]

Issues for Congress

Maritime territorial and EEZ disputes in the SCS and ECS involving China raise several potential policy and oversight issues for Congress, including those discussed below.

U.S. Strategy for Countering "Salami-Slicing" Strategy

Particularly in light of the potential implications for the United States if China were to achieve domination over or control of its near-seas areas (see previous section), one potential oversight issue for Congress concerns the U.S. strategy for countering China's "salami-slicing" strategy. Potential oversight questions for Congress include the following:

---

[77] Navy Office of Legislative Affairs email to CRS dated September 4, 2012. Similarly, some observers have argued that China's position regarding the SCS and ECS is similar to the U.S. Monroe Doctrine for Latin America in the 19th and early-20th centuries. In response to this argument, one observer states that

> China's policy in the near seas today bears scant resemblance to U.S. policy in the Caribbean and Gulf in the age of the Monroe Doctrine. For one thing, Washington never asserted title to the Caribbean the way Beijing claims the South China Sea. For another, America never sought to restrict naval activities in its near seas, whereas China opposes such things as routine aircraft carrier operations in the Yellow Sea.... In effect, China has vaulted past the most bellicose, most meddlesome interpretations of the Monroe Doctrine and Roosevelt Corollary.

> (James Holmes, "China's Monroe Doctrine," *The Diplomat* (http://thediplomat.com), June 22, 2012, accessed November 21, 2012, at http://thediplomat.com/2012/06/22/chinas-monroe-doctrine/

[78] Department of Defense, *Annual Report to Congress [on] Military and Security Developments Involving the People's Republic of China 2013*, p. 39.

- Does the United States have a strategy for countering China's "salami-slicing" strategy?

- If the United States does have such a strategy, what are its key elements, and has it been effective? Should the strategy be changed, and if so, how?

- If the United States does not have such a strategy, does the Administration intend to create one, and if so, by when?

Comments by Some Observers on Whether the United States Has a Strategy

One observer states:

> Salami-slicing places rivals, especially conflicted rivals, in an uncomfortable position. It is the rivals of salami-slicers who are obligated to eventually draw red lines and engage in brinkmanship over actions others will view, in isolation, as trivial and far from constituting casus belli. China's leaders are apparently counting on such hesitancy, a calculation that thus far is working out for them....
>
> ... there is no visible response by the U.S. government to China's salami-slicing. U.S. officials... have expressed regret over China's ADIZ declaration, and stated their intention to carry on with usual U.S. military operations inside that zone and elsewhere in the region. Yet China has suffered no penalty for its series of actions. Regarding the disputed claims in the two seas, the official policy from Washington is that China's neighbors are on their own—the U.S. will not take sides in these territorial disputes. The United States also objects to the use of coercion in resolving the disputes. But each individual act of China's salami-slicing is carefully calibrated to fall below a threshold most outside observers would view as overt coercion.
>
> With no resistance to its actions, Chinese salami-slicing will certainly continue....
>
> When the salami-slices sum up to a substantial security problem for Japan, India, and the ASEAN countries, someone is likely to draw a red line somewhere. The issue for U.S. officials is whether they will be the ones to do that drawing, and thus retain the initiative, or whether someone else, having lost confidence in Washington, will do it instead. When that happens, the U.S. will find itself reacting to events, rather than shaping a favorable outcome in advance.[79]

Another observer states that

> the problem with [the U.S. military's Air-Sea Battle, or ASB, concept] (and its main competitors) is that they are only designed for high-level conflict, and thus can only be implemented if the U.S. and China move from a state of tense peace to a state of total war. In other words, unless China takes a brazenly provocative action such as invading Taiwan or parts of Japan, ASB is more or less useless. No U.S. president is going to order the U.S. military to take the extremely provocative actions that ASB would require because of, say, recent actions by China setting up an oil rig in waters that it disputes with Vietnam.

---

[79] Robert Haddick, "America Has No Answer to China's Salami-Slicing," *War on the Rocks* (http://warontherocks.com), February 6, 2014.

This is problematic. Thus far, China's military strategy for the South and East China Seas has been one of using salami-slicing tactics to gradually change facts on the ground. In the face of these salami-slicing tactics, ASB is of complete irrelevance.

Moreover, China's salami-slicing tactics appear to be working. It has already gained control over Scarborough Shoal from the Philippines, and appears poised to do the same in the Second Thomas Shoal. Its claims to waters around the Paracel Islands are now strengthening further out from Hainan Island with Beijing's recent oil-rig gambit in South China Sea, and its routine patrols of the Senkaku/Diaoyu Islands are now an accepted fact on the ground.

As long as these salami-slicing tactics continue to yield results, it seems unimaginable that Beijing will resort to the brazen actions that would reasonably trigger an ASB response from Washington. Thus, for ASB to regain a sense of relevance, the United States and its allies must first find an answer to Beijing's salami-slicing tactics. Put differently: until China finds it cannot achieve its goals through salami slicing, it will not resort to the higher spectrum conflict that ASB was designed to deter or defeat.[80]

Another observer states that

Until quite recently, China's aggressive moves in the South China Sea were widely viewed as the product of an erratic foreign policy driven by competing agencies in which hawkish players usually came out on top....

But the latest Chinese moves that have so alarmed the U.S. and China's neighbors... appear to be the result not of policy confusion but deliberate planning, say Chinese and foreign security analysts. They are most likely coordinated at the highest level. Ultimately, they seem to bear the stamp of the country's president, Xi Jinping....

On the surface, this may look reckless. But one theory gaining traction among senior officials and policy analysts around Asia and in Washington is that the timing is well calculated. It reflects Mr. Xi's belief that he is dealing with a weak U.S. president who won't push back, despite his strong rhetorical support for Asian allies.

Mr. Xi's perception, say these analysts, has been heightened by U.S. President Barack Obama's failure to intervene militarily in Syria and Ukraine. And it's led him to conclude that he has a window of opportunity to aggresively assert China's territorial claims around the region.[81]

Two other observers state that

what is happening in the South China Sea is actually far more dangerous than what has come before—and the forces driving it go well beyond pursuit of energy riches. The United States needs to face up to the full magnitude of the Chinese challenge to have any hope of successfully confronting it. This means not only tough talk but also a willingness to take difficult action....

The United States has said it won't take a stand on the sovereignty dispute and has called on the two parties to resolve their differences peacefully. This is not enough: The United States ought to call China's bluff and make clear the real stakes. The United States and the

---

[80] Zachary Keck, "Is Air-Sea Battle Useless?" *The National Interest* (http://nationalinterest.org), May 16, 2014.

[81] Andrew Browne, "Beijing Moves Boldly, Calculates Carefully," *Wall Street Journal* (http://online.wsj.com), June 3, 2014.

Association of Southeast Asian Nations (ASEAN) should present a unified front in refusing to recognize unilateral assertions of claims in disputed territories.

Even more important, the United States must be prepared to give life to its rhetorical position. Although it does not have a treaty obligation to defend Vietnam, its rebalancing to Asia is premised on its role as the primary guarantor of stability in the Pacific. Chinese actions challenge that.

Vietnam has reiterated its commitment to peacefully resolve the dispute. If China does not reciprocate, the United States should be prepared to offer support to Vietnam through an increased naval presence. This would give Washington the ability to assess Chinese capabilities and to help de-escalate the situation. Other options, such as restrictions on CNOOC's activities in the United States, could also be considered. If the United States can't back up its words with actions, its credibility in promising to uphold peace and stability in the region will be gutted.[82]

Another observer states:

These are times of mounting drama and tension in the long power play of China's rise in Asia. Thus, it is more important than ever for American policy makers to peer behind the curtain to see when rising-power loneliness is dressed as leadership and when confidence is a mask for insecurity....

The Asian strategic order may now be in play; its U.S.-led character is under question, but this is a complex, multilayered game. If China is seeking to rattle America and others—especially Japan, the Philippines and Vietnam—it may be miscalculating. In the long run, the premature displays of confidence China has lately shown are likely to harm its interests more than advance them....

Under question is the region's capacity to craft an order that is at once stable and free from domination by a single power. If China's latest behavior and rhetoric can partly be explained by an excess of the wrong sort of confidence—premature, misjudged or a conduit for nationalism—then the United States, its allies and partners will need to be firm, yet also careful and nimble, in how they push back. Somehow, the message needs to reach China's security decision makers that their continued risk-taking could have consequences they cannot control.

What the region requires is a new kind of balance—not of power or of resolve, but of uncertainty. Of late, too much of the uncertainty has been in the minds of America's Asian allies and partners. Turning this situation around may be a first step towards China's acceptance that it will have to live up to its 'win-win' rhetoric when dealing with all its neighbors. In other words, what is needed now is greater uncertainty among China's strategic decision makers about how the United States, Japan and the region's middle powers will respond to—or anticipate—the next coercive move.

Beijing may pretend to shrug off one legal action, but will have trouble sustaining its indifference if Vietnam or additional South China Sea claimants also seek international arbitration with the overt blessing of the United States, the European Union and other champions of a rules-based international system. Stability in the South China Sea, a global shipping artery, is every trading nation's business. So Washington would be well advised to

---

[82] Elizabeth Economy and Michael Levi, "Beijing's Actions in the South China Sea Demand A U.S. Response," *Washington Post (www.washingtonpost.com)*, May 15, 2014.

follow the kind of practical action plan recently advanced by security policy expert Ely Ratner, involving a coordinated assertion of rules-based management of maritime disputes, globally through the G7, as well as regionally through the East Asia Summit [see next item below]. Simultaneously, the United States and its allies, including Japan, are in their rights to signal that they will expand security capacity-building, training and intelligence-sharing when Southeast Asian states invite them to do so in response to new anxieties about China's actions.

Shifting the balance of uncertainty in Asia need not have a principally military dimension. Even with constrained resources, the U.S. Navy can sustain a visible presence in the South China Sea and, by invitation, in the territorial seas and exclusive economic zones of partners and allies. New anxieties about regional stability will encourage more countries to join U.S.-led maritime exercises and surveillance cooperation throughout the Indo-Pacific. This need not amount to provocation, if combined with persistent invitations for China to begin serious risk-reduction dialogue so that close encounters like the December 2013 USS Cowpens incident become less likely to occur or escalate. The truth is, China's maritime assertiveness in recent years has not risen relentlessly. Notably, the tempo of sea and air incidents against Japan—though still troubling—has eased this year; the disciplined pushback by Japan's experienced maritime forces may well be a factor. Beneath the bluster, at least some of China's security actors must know they cannot be the masters of infinite risk. This will be a long drama and the script is not theirs alone to write.[83]

Another observer states:

American aspirations for China's rise have gone terribly off-script. For decades, U.S. policy toward China has comprised a dual-track "hedging" strategy that includes engaging Beijing in an effort to induce China to support the existing international order, accompanied by a balancing component in which the United States and its allies deter Beijing from choosing an aggressive path. But now this strategy is coming apart at both ends: China neither accepts the territorial realities of Asia, nor is it deterred from coercive acts of revisionism.

The real problem is that China's bullying will endure as long as no one gets in the way. Why wouldn't it? Beijing is pushing on an open door, incurring few tangible costs for its assertiveness and appearing to believe (perhaps rightly so) that it can ride out whatever regional criticism arises in response. Based on its track record of the last several years, it's understandable that Beijing remains confident that most countries in the region will, at the end of the day, be unwilling to imperil their economic relationship with China.

Alarm bells ought be ringing more loudly in Washington. Ultimately, it will be up to the United States to staunch China's mounting revisionism. But this will first require a sober recognition that the old theories of how to shape China's rise aren't working. This is a difficult conversation to have in Washington because acknowledging Chinese behavior for what it is—undeterred and unapologetic assertiveness—will necessitate a more serious American response than we have seen to date.

This doesn't mean forgoing the cooperative elements of the "hedge" and committing to a highly competitive relationship with China. We're not there yet. And besides, there's a big difference between determining that China is presently undeterred versus determining that it is patently undeterrable. Before definitively drawing the latter conclusion, the immediate task for U.S. policymakers is to test the elasticity of Chinese decision-making.

---

[83] Rory Medcalf, "China's Premature Power Play Goes Very Wrong," *The National Interest* (http://nationalinterest.org), June 3, 2014.

This calls for greater attention to cost-imposition strategies that attempt to shape the relative value of continued revisionism for China. Washington will have to explore the full potential range of economic, military, diplomatic and political points of leverage over Beijing (and there are many) to increase the costs of Chinese assertiveness, including areas that directly impinge on the interests of China's leaders. The United States will also have to develop more tailored options for responding directly to maritime coercion in ways that repel specific acts of revisionism, rather than simply exacting lateral forms of punishment after the fact.

China's slow but steady revisions to the territorial status quo in Asia are not a legacy the Obama administration wants to leave behind. Being more proactive in stemming this behavior represents the principal challenge for Washington's China policy today.[84]

Another observer states:

In the case of China trying to support its territorial claims, I think there's an upper limit on what it will do. Below that limit, though, the Chinese are sitting around, thinking, "Now, what can I do next? Let's see, I can extend the ADIZ (Air Defense Identification Zone), I can declare a new fishing zone, etc. ...."

They're coming up with all sorts of gray-zone challenges, and they're going to keep on doing so. We have to figure out how to counter those actions. You can't just sit there and react to what the Chinese are doing. Of course, you need to think them through carefully, but if the Chinese want to play a game of "I'll poke you here, and I'll poke you there," then you have to respond and say, "Game on." Japan, the Philippines and Vietnam need to take initiatives of their own and be equally forceful in that space.[85]

Comments by Some Observers Suggesting Elements of a U.S. Strategy

One observer, proposing series of actions for the United States to take during the summer months of 2014, states:

It's time to breathe new life into U.S. policy in the South China Sea. Despite important initiatives by the Obama administration to strengthen bilateral security ties, build partner capacity and enhance multilateral cooperation, the region's territorial and maritime disputes continue to engender dangerous crises. The potential for armed conflict will only grow larger in the absence of creative and decisive U.S. leadership....

The costs for the United States of failing to play an innovative leadership role could be enormous. Against this backdrop, the coming months provide a series of critical opportunities for top-level U.S. officials to evolve and advance U.S. policy. Below is a proposed calendar for launching four new initiatives that are practical, feasible and would support U.S. interests in the region....

At the Shangri-La Dialogue in Singapore at the end of May, Secretary Hagel should propose in concept the development of a multilateral MDA initiative. In concert, the National Security Council staff should lead an interagency working group to offer recommendations related to cost, operational requirements and intelligence sharing. The administration should

---

[84] Ely Ratner, "China Undeterred and Unapologetic," *War on the Rocks (http://warontherocks)*, June 24, 2014. See also Ely Ratner, "A Plan to Counter Chinese Aggression," *Wall Street Journal (http://online.wsj.com)*, June 10, 2014.

[85] Yoichi Kato, "Interview: Dennis Blair: China Containing Itself By Aggressive Actions In Region," *Asahi Shimbun (http://ajw.asahi.com)*, June 26, 2014. Ellipse as in original.

also consider potential groupings of allies and partners, including (but not limited to) an ASEAN-centered architecture....

At the G-7 summit in Brussels in June, President Obama should propose to include language in the summit's joint statement supporting the legitimacy of international arbitration to manage maritime disputes in the South China Sea....

Beginning at the U.S.-China Strategic Security Dialogue in August, the United States should make clear in private that it expects China to withdraw its occupation of the disputed feature by the end of 2014 and return to the pre-April 2012 status quo. If necessary, this message can be repeated publicly in ASEAN-centered regional forums later in the year, including the East Asia Summit in Burma in November. The United States military should also consider conducting freedom of navigation operations in areas surrounding the reef to underscore that the United States does not recognize Chinese administration....

Secretary Kerry should propose the idea of an "early harvest" of the COC at the ASEAN Regional Forum in August and, with guidance from the U.S. Mission to ASEAN in Jakarta, propose specific components of the COC discussions that are widely agreed-upon and ripe for immediate implementation.[86]

Two other observers, proposing a U.S. strategy for the South China Sea, states:

The United States should develop and promulgate a National Strategy for the South China Sea (NSSCS) as part of its ongoing efforts to counter Chinese aggression in the region and to resolve the disputes there in a peaceful manner. It behooves the United States to shift its current posture in the South China Sea from one of vigilant maintenance of the status quo to a position that will foster the peaceful management and ultimately permanent resolution of issues affecting U.S. navigational rights and interests in the region. An NSSCS is one effective means of producing the necessary shift....

Specifically, the U.S. should:

1. Take an official position regarding disputed SCS land features....

2. Underscore U.S. policy on military activities in the SCS....

3. Continue freedom-of-navigation protests and naval operations....

4. Publish a "Limits in the Seas" report regarding the nine-dash line....

5. Assist SCS nations in complying with the law of the sea....

6. Support arbitration cases against China....

7. Preempt potentially harmful provisions of an SCS "code of conduct."[87]

Another observer, proposing U.S. actions for helping Vietnam to Counter China's claims in tghe SCS, states:

---

[86] Ely Ratner, A Summer Calendar for Advancing U.S. Policy toward the South China Sea, Center for a New American Security, May 2014, pp. 1-8.

[87] Steven Groves and Dean Cheng, *A National Strategy for the South China Sea, Heritage Foundation*, April 24, 2014 (Backgrounder No. 2908), pp. 1, 11-13.

Beijing is opportunistically seeking to flex its newfound muscle and make the 9-dash line a *de facto* and *de jure* reality. In effect, China wants the South (and East) China Sea as an inland lake. The placement of [the] HS-981 [oil rig] is part of a disturbing pattern of aggressive Chinese behavior. Another ongoing resort to "tailored coercion" is the reclamation of small land features in the Spratly Islands. Recently released photographs taken in March show China's reclamation of Johnson South Reef, the site of a 1988 Vietnam-China naval skirmish. Although China is not alone is seeking to advance its territorial claims and maritime interests, its behavior is uniquely escalatory. US Secretary of Defense Chuck Hagel singled out China's "destabilizing, unilateral actions" against its maritime neighbors at this year's Shangri-La Dialogue in Singapore.

The placement of [the] HS-981 [oil rig], coming after diplomatic exertions to improve Beijing-Hanoi ties, is perplexing to many in the region. But China's gambit in its near seas involves dialing up and dialing down coercive diplomacy. As part of a renewed focus on "periphery diplomacy," China is rewarding neighbors willing to work with Beijing, and is seeking to isolate those who resist China's unilateral demands. Such actions are tailored to be sufficiently peaceful so as not to escalate into full-fledged conflict or to trigger a unified, anti-China alliance; they are tailored to appear sufficiently non-military in nature and thus not intended to accentuate China's rapidly modernizing military forces; and they are tailored to send varying messages to different audiences—internal, regional, and international. China's tailored coercion is aimed not just at its neighbors but also at the United States. China wants to coerce the United States to tamp down the national exuberance of its allies and partners, from the Philippines and Japan (in the East China Sea), to Vietnam and Malaysia. Notwithstanding China's coercive behavior, the United States needs to persevere in building an open, rules-based system in the Asia-Pacific region. But in the meantime, it also needs to find a way to address Chinese incremental aggression, often likened to salami slicing. In the present SCS crisis, the United States needs to bolster its ties with Vietnam to help impose costs on China. Taking together the twin US goals of regional security maintenance and order building, and focusing on countering China's use of coercion to unilaterally alter the status quo, there are five priorities that deserve attention from both Hanoi and Washington, and the region in general.

First, as part of the burgeoning US-Vietnam security dialogue, the two countries should focus on developing cost-imposition strategies that might dissuade China from resorting to unilateral changes to the status quo or impose stiff penalties for bad behavior. Cost-imposition strategies can be direct and indirect, military and non-military, short-term and long-term. But they should be feasible, cost-effective, and meaningful. Vietnam needs to send top-level officials to Washington to underscore the importance of this dialogue.

Second, there should be more frequent and larger bilateral exercises and US military deployments to Vietnam under the existing shared membership in the Proliferation Security Initiative (PSI). Through PSI, the United States can provide a reassuring presence without taking on the burdens, costs and risks of trying to restore a permanent military base. At the same time, greater US-Vietnam cooperation can improve the professionalism of Vietnamese defenses and the capacity for combined action. Improving maritime domain awareness is an objective that supports both PSI and would have benefits for the early detection of misbehavior in the East Sea.

Third, the United States should support triangular dialogue and practical cooperation among other SCS claimant states, especially Vietnam, Malaysia and the Philippines. The United States can support this dialogue through regional multilateral forums such as the ASEAN Regional Forum, the ASEAN Defense Ministers' Meeting Plus and the East Asia Summit. Washington can also encourage other US allies and partners (Japan, South Korea, Australia, India and other members of ASEAN) to offer assistance with training and education, equipment and information sharing. The United States should encourage Japan, which is already providing coast guard patrol vessels beginning next year, and India, which operates Russian submarines, to assist the Vietnamese navy to operate and deploy Russian Kilo-class submarines. As Vietnam incorporates six submarines into its small navy, others need to help Vietnam establish operational independence.

Fourth, the United States should end the ban on lethal arms sales to Vietnam. The scope and kind of direct military support can still be linked to demonstrable improvements in human rights. But it is now time to begin limited arms sales that are useful for countering tailored coercion. Such systems could improve maritime domain awareness and bolster defensive if still potentially lethal means of punishing any attacker. Torpedoes and short-range cruise missiles would strengthen deterrence, and a potential aggressor would think twice before using overt coercion or limited force to make its claims.

Fifth, the United States should press Vietnam and other ASEAN members to support specific rules for maintaining good order at sea and preserve the freedom of the global commons in the South China Sea. Specific steps that might eventually be part of a binding code of conduct should be promoted and put into practice as soon as possible. International arbitration over UNCLOS provisions should be embraced. Land features should be systematically cataloged and defined to develop a shared regional understanding of what land features are islands and which are rocks.

These steps are illustrative of a broader tool kit at the disposal of officials in Vietnam, the United States and the region to impose costs on bad behavior and provide safeguards for complying with mutually agreed rules. They are necessary because of China's increasing reliance on coercion. At the same time, it is vital to further develop a roadmap with China on how to avert dangerous incidents and manage strategic competition. Through these steps, tailored coercion can be prevented from becoming the accepted norm in the South China Sea.[88]

Some Reported U.S. Actions

A December 16, 2013, State Department fact sheet states:

> On December 16, Secretary of State John Kerry announced an initial commitment of $32.5 million in new regional and bilateral assistance to advance maritime capacity building in Southeast Asia. Including this new funding, our planned region-wide funding support for maritime capacity building exceeds $156 million for the next two years.
>
> As an example of our commitment to strengthen maritime capacities in Southeast Asia, the United States intends to provide up to $18 million in new assistance to Vietnam to enhance the capacity of coastal patrol units to deploy rapidly for search and rescue, disaster response, and other activities, including through provision of five fast patrol vessels in 2014 to the Vietnamese Coast Guard. This assistance directly responds to priorities identified in the Joint Minutes on Vietnam and U.S. Coast Guard Maritime Cooperation signed October 1, 2013, by VCG Major General Nguyen Quang Dam and USCG Commandant Admiral Robert J. Papp, Jr.
>
> The United States will also expand its support for regional cooperation by strengthening information sharing among national agencies in Southeast Asia charged with maritime security and maritime law enforcement. Building on existing programs and initiatives, we

---

[88] Patrick M. Cronin, "US Should Help Vietnam Counter China's Coercion," *Asia Pacific Bulletin (www.eastwestcenter.org)*, Number 269, June 26, 2014. Italics as in original.

will increase training for maritime law enforcement officials from participating Southeast Asian countries in multilateral settings, such as currently occurs in the Gulf of Thailand initiative and Trilateral Interagency Maritime Law Enforcement Workshops. We will take advantage of the International Law Enforcement Academy in Bangkok, Thailand, to deliver new maritime law enforcement training courses for maritime officials across Southeast Asia.

The Secretary's announcement builds upon the United States' longstanding commitment to support the efforts of Southeast Asian nations to enhance security and prosperity in the region, including in the maritime domain. Existing programs include efforts to combat piracy in and around the Malacca Strait, to counter transnational organized crime and terrorist threats in the tri-border region south of the Sulu Sea between the southern Philippines, Indonesia, and Malaysia, and to expand information sharing and professional training through the Gulf of Thailand initiative. In addition, since 1999 the U.S.-supported International Law Enforcement Academy in Bangkok, Thailand has been one of the world's premier multilateral platforms for law enforcement training and cooperation.[89]

A March 30, 2014, press report states:

Japan and the United States plan to create a permanent consultative body to coordinate the operations of the Self-Defense Forces and the U.S. military in the face of China's highhanded actions over the Senkaku Islands in Okinawa Prefecture, Japanese and U.S. government sources said.

The envisaged body is expected to help Japan and the United States deal quickly with situations in and around the islands that cannot be clearly identified as armed attacks, the sources said.

Establishment of the consultative body will be included in revisions to the Guidelines for Japan-U.S. Defense Cooperation scheduled for the end of the year....

During their talks to review the current guidelines, foreign and defense officials from both sides stated that there is a need to create a permanent coordination body when they went over desktop military exercises and exchanged opinions on how quasi-military attacks on Japan should be handled.

Experts predict that an attempt by China to seize the Senkakus would very likely begin with the landing of armed personnel disguised as fishermen. The prediction has prompted the Japanese side to demand enhancement of the Japan-U.S. partnership to deal with such ambiguous situations.[90]

In assessing the question of U.S. strategy for countering China's salami-slicing strategy, one potential matter that Congress may consider concerns the relatively limited ability of the Philippines' to patrol its EEZ, which includes Scarborough Shoal and some of the Spratly Islands (see **Figure 4**), and to otherwise assert and defend its maritime claims. The Philippines has relatively few modern ships larger than patrol craft in its navy or coast guard, and the country's resulting limited capability for patrolling the EEZ and otherwise asserting and defending its

---

[89] Department of State Fact Sheet, "Expanded U.S. Assistance for Maritime Capacity Building," December 16, 2013, accessed March 14, 2013, at http://www.state.gov/r/pa/prs/ps/2013/218735 htm.

[90] Takashi Imai, "Japan, US To Create New Defense Body For Disputed Islands," *Stars and Stripes* (*www.stripes.com*), March 30, 2014, accessed April 9, 2014, at http://www.stripes.com/news/pacific/japan-us-to-create-new-defense-body-for-disputed-islands-1.275417.

maritime claims can be viewed as contributing to a power vacuum in the SCS that China can exploit in asserting and defending its maritime territorial claims in the area.[91]

The United States has taken certain actions to improve the Philippines' ability for patrolling its EEZ and otherwise asserting and defending its maritime claims, including the transfer of two ex-U.S. Coast Guard Hamilton-class cutters to the Philippines' navy. The United States and the Philippines have also signed an agreement that will provide increased access to Philippine bases for U.S. forces. The Philippines also plans to acquire two new frigates from Italy, a used frigate from South Korea,[92] 10 patrol boats from Japan, and additional aircraft.[93] Whether these and other additions will give the Philippines a sufficient capability for patrolling its EEZ and otherwise asserting and defending its maritime claims is not clear. Potential follow-on questions for Congress include the following:

- Will the Philippines' current plans for acquiring new ships and aircraft give the Philippines a sufficient capability for patrolling its EEZ and otherwise asserting and defending its maritime claims?

- If not, what would be the potential advantages or disadvantages of initiating a U.S. or multilateral program for providing the Philippines with additional ships and aircraft? What might such a program look like? As part of its FY2015 budget submission, for example, the U.S. Navy is proposing to retire all 10 of its remaining Oliver Hazard Perry (FFG-7) class frigates. Other ships in this class that have been removed from U.S. Navy service have in some cases have been transferred to other countries. Should some or all of these 10 frigates be transferred to the Philippines as part of a program that also provided support for training crews and for establishing logistics and maintenance support facilities for these ships?

Risk of United States Being Drawn Into a Crisis or Conflict

Another potential issue for Congress concerns U.S. actions to reduce the risk that the United States might be drawn into a crisis or conflict over a territorial dispute involving China. Potential oversight questions for Congress include the following:

- Have U.S. officials taken appropriate and sufficient steps to help reduce the risk of maritime territorial disputes in the SCS and ECS escalating into conflicts?

- Do the United States and Japan have a common understanding of potential U.S. actions under Article IV of the U.S.-Japan Treaty on Mutual Cooperation and Security in the event of a crisis or conflict over the Senkaku Islands? What steps has the United States taken to ensure that the two countries share a common understanding?

---

[91] Limitations on Vietnamese and Malaysian capabilities can also be viewed as contributing to such a power vacuum; for a discussion, see Nah Liang Tuang, "China's Maritime Expansion: Exploiting Regional Weakness?" *The Diplomat* (http://thediplomat.com), March 5, 2014.

[92] Ridzwan Rahmat, "Philippines to Receive Retired South Korean Corvette," *IHS Jane's 360 (www.janes.com)*, June 8, 2014.

[93] For a discussion, see, for example, Trefor Moss, "Aboard the Philippine Navy's Newest Old Frigate," *Wall Street Journal (http://blogs.wsj.com)*, July 2, 2014.

- Do the United States and the Philippines have a common understanding of how the 1951 U.S.-Philippines mutual defense treaty applies to maritime territories in the SCS that are claimed by both China and the Philippines, and of potential U.S. actions under Article IV of the treaty in the event of a crisis or conflict over the territories? What steps has the United States taken to ensure that the two countries share a common understanding?

- Aside from public statements, what has the United States communicated to China regarding potential U.S. actions under the two treaties in connection with maritime territorial disputes in the SCS and ECS?

- Has the United States correctly balanced ambiguity and explicitness in its communications to various parties regarding potential U.S. actions under the two defense treaties?

- How do the two treaties affect the behavior of Japan, the Philippines, and China in managing their territorial disputes? To what extent, for example, would they help Japan or the Philippines resist potential Chinese attempts to resolve the disputes through intimidation, or, alternatively, encourage risk-taking or brinksmanship behavior by Japan or the Philippines in their dealings with China on the disputes? To what extent do they deter or limit Chinese assertiveness or aggressiveness in their dealings with Japan the Philippines on the disputes?

- Has the DOD adequately incorporated into its planning crisis and conflict scenarios arising from maritime territorial disputes in the SCS and ECS that fall under the terms of the two treaties?

Whether United States Should Enter Into A U.S.-Chinese Incidents-at-Sea (INCSEA) Agreement

Another potential issue for Congress is whether the United States should seek to reduce the risk of future incidents between U.S. and Chinese ships and aircraft in China's EEZ by entering into an agreement with China regulating the behavior of U.S. Chinese ships and aircraft that are operating in proximity with one another. Such an agreement could be broadly similar to the May 1972 U.S.-Soviet agreement on the prevention of incidents on and over the high seas, commonly known as the Incidents-at-Sea (INCSEA) agreement.[94]

Supporters of this option could argue the following:

- The May 1972 U.S.-Soviet INCSEA agreement is regarded by observers as having been successful in helping to reduce the risk of incidents between U.S. and Soviet ships and aircraft during the Cold War.

- A broadly similar agreement with China could reduce the risk of incidents involving U.S. and Chinese ships and aircraft, and could be useful in that regard as a confidence-building measure.

---

[94] 23 UST 1168; TIAS 7379; UNTS 151. The agreement was signed at Moscow on May 25, 1972, and entered into force the same day.

- The terms of such an agreement could be drafted to be consistent with the U.S. position on whether a coastal state has the right to regulate foreign military forces operating in their EEZs.

Opponents of this option could argue the following:

- When the May 1972 U.S.-Soviet INCSEA agreement was signed, the October 1972 multilateral convention on the international regulations for preventing collisions at sea (commonly known as the COLREGs or the "rules of the road")[95] (see discussion in "Background") did not yet exist. In contrast to the situation in May 1972, the COLREGs convention now exists, and both China and the United States are party to it. China and the United States are also party to the 2014 Code for Unplanned Encounters at Sea (CUES) and the 1998 bilateral U.S.-Chinese Military Maritime Consultative Agreement (MMCA), which is aimed at reducing the chances of confrontation between the two countries' militaries at sea and in the air.[96] Managing U.S.-Chinese interactions at sea requires standards to govern conduct and a forum to discuss incidents. A new INCSEA-like agreement is not necessary, because both of these things are already in place: The COLREGs and CUES provide the standards, and the consultative mechanism created by the MMCA creates the forum.

- Chinese vessels arguably violated both the COLREGs and Article 94 of UNCLOS in the 2009 incident with a U.S. ship.[97] The Chinese ship involved in the December 5, 2013, incident involving the *Cowpens* might have violated the COLREGs.[98] Consequently, signing a new INCSEA-like agreement with China could be viewed as rewarding China for past violations and be of questionable value in preventing future U.S.-Chinese incidents at sea.[99]

Related potential oversight questions for Congress include the following:

- Is the number of countries that share China's view on whether coastal states have a right under UNCLOS to regulate the activities of foreign military forces in their EEZs growing, and if so, what steps is the Administration taking to stop or

---

[95] 28 UST 3459; TIAS 8587. The treaty was done at London October 20, 1972, and entered into force July 15, 1977. A summary of the agreement is available at http://www.imo.org/about/conventions/listofconventions/pages/colreg.aspx.

[96] For more on the MMCA, see CRS Report RL32496, *U.S.-China Military Contacts: Issues for Congress*, by Shirley A. Kan.

[97] For a detailed argument that the behavior of Chinese ships in the March 2009 U.S.-Chinese incident at sea in China's EEZ violated the COLREGs and Article 94 of UNCLOS, see Jonathan G. Odom, "The True 'Lies' of the *Impeccable* Incident: What Really Happened, Who Disregarded International Law, and Why Every Nation (Outside of China) Should Be Concerned," *Michigan State Journal of International Law*, vol. 18, no. 3, 2010: 16-22. Accessed September 25, 2012, at http://papers.ssrn.com/sol3/papers.cfm?abstract_id=1622943.

[98] As noted earlier (see "1972 Multilateral Convention on Preventing Collisions at Sea (COLREGs Convention)"), DOD states that "The PLA Navy vessel's action was inconsistent with internationally recognized rules concerning professional maritime behavior (i.e., the Convention of International Regulations for Preventing Collisions at Sea), to which China is a party." (Department of Defense, *Annual Report to Congress [on] Military and Security Developments Involving the People's Republic of China 2014*, p. 4.)

[99] For additional discussion, see China's Active Defense Strategy and its Regional Impact, Prepared statement by Stacy A. Pedrozo, CAPT, JAGC, USN1, U.S. Navy Military Fellow, Council on Foreign Relations, Before the U.S.-China Economic & Security Review Commission, United States House of Representatives, First Session, 112th Congress, January 27, 2011, p. 8. (The title page mistakenly shows a date of January 27, 2010.) See also Bonnie S. Glaser, *Armed Clash in the South China Sea*, Council on Foreign Relations, Center for Preventive Action, April 2012, pp. 4-5.)

reverse this growth? What activities is the Administration taking, vis-a-vis China or other countries, to reinforce the U.S. position on whether coastal states have a right under UNCLOS to regulate the activities of foreign military forces in their EEZs?

- One of the 27 countries listed earlier (see "Dispute Regarding China's Rights Within Its EEZ") as having restrictions inconsistent with UNCLOS that would limit the exercise of high seas freedoms by foreign navies beyond 12 nautical miles from the coast is Portugal. Given Portugal's status as a NATO ally and a historical maritime power, to what extent do Portugal's restrictions make it more difficult for the United States to defend its position on the question of whether coastal states have the right to regulate foreign military activities in their EEZs? What steps has the Administration taken to encourage Portugal, as a NATO ally that derives collective security benefits from U.S. defense efforts, to end its restrictions and affirm the U.S. position on the question of whether coastal states have the right to regulate foreign military activities in their EEZs?

- Another one of the 27 countries listed earlier is Thailand—a country with a coast on the Gulf of Thailand, a body of water that opens onto the South China Sea. Given Thailand's status as the United States' oldest ally in Southeast Asia (as described by DOD) and as the host country for the annual Cobra Gold exercise, the United States' longest-standing military exercise in the Pacific,[100] what steps has the Administration taken to encourage Thailand to end its restrictions that would limit the exercise of high seas freedoms by foreign navies beyond 12 nautical miles from the coast and affirm the U.S. position on the question of whether coastal states have the right to regulate foreign military activities in their EEZs?

- Another one of the 27 listed earlier is Vietnam—a country whose relations with the United States have improved in recent years, in part because of China's activities in the SCS. What steps has the Administration taken to encourage Vietnam to end its restrictions that would limit the exercise of high seas freedoms by foreign navies beyond 12 nautical miles from the coast and affirm the U.S. position on the question of whether coastal states have the right to regulate foreign military activities in their EEZs?

- China in recent years has begun to operate small numbers of navy ships in the Indian Ocean (for anti-piracy operations), the Persian Gulf, and the Mediterranean Sea. Chinese officials are also concerned about the security of their maritime oil supply routes from the Persian Gulf. To what extent have U.S. officials communicated to Chinese officials that, in light of these developments, China arguably has an increasing interest in changing its position on whether coastal states have a right under UNCLOS to regulate the activities of foreign military forces in their EEZs?

---

[100] Source: Donna Miles, "Cobra Gold 2012 to Promote Partnership, Interoperability," *American Forces Press Service (DOD)*, accessed September 25, 2012, at http://www.defense.gov/news/newsarticle.aspx?id=66803.)

Whether United States Should Ratify United Nations Convention on the Law of the Sea (UNCLOS)

Another issue for Congress—particularly the Senate—is the impact of maritime territorial and EEZ disputes involving China on the overall debate on whether the United States should become a party to UNCLOS. UNCLOS was adopted by Third United Nations Conference on the Law of the Sea in December 1982, and entered into force in November 1994. The treaty established EEZs as a feature of international law, and contains multiple provisions relating to territorial waters and EEZs. As of September 21, 2012, 162 nations were party to the treaty, including China and most other countries bordering on the SCS and ECS (the exceptions being North Korea and Taiwan).[101]

The treaty and an associated 1994 agreement relating to implementation of Part XI of the treaty (on deep seabed mining) were transmitted to the Senate on October 6, 1994.[102] In the absence of Senate advice and consent to adherence, the United States is not a party to the convention and the associated 1994 agreement. During the 112th Congress, the Senate Foreign Relations Committee held four hearings on the question of whether the United States should become a party to the treaty on May 23, June 14 (two hearings), and June 28, 2012.

Supporters of the United States becoming a party to UNCLOS argue or might argue one or more of the following:

- The treaty's provisions relating to navigational rights, including those in EEZs, reflect the U.S. position on the issue; becoming a party to the treaty would help lock the U.S. perspective into permanent international law.

- Becoming a party to the treaty would give the United States greater standing for participating in discussions relating to the treaty—a "seat at the table"—and thereby improve the U.S. ability to call on China to act in accordance with the treaty's provisions, including those relating to navigational rights, and to defend U.S. interpretations of the treaty's provisions, including those relating to whether coastal states have a right under UNCLOS to regulate foreign military activities in their EEZs.[103]

- At least some of the ASEAN member states want the United States to become a member of UNCLOS, because they view it as the principal framework for resolving maritime territorial disputes.

- Relying on customary international law to defend U.S. interests in these issues is not sufficient, because it is not universally accepted and is subject to change over time based on state practice.

---

[101] Source: Chronological lists of ratifications of, accessions and successions to the Convention and the related Agreements as at 21 September 2012, accessed September 26, 2012, at http://www.un.org/Depts/los/reference_files/ chronological_lists_of_ratifications htm#The United Nations Convention on the Law of the Sea. A similar list, in alphabetical order by country name, is posted at http://www.un.org/Depts/los/reference_files/status2010.pdf.

[102] Treaty Document 103-39.

[103] See, for example, Andrew Browne, "A Hole in the U.S. Approach to Beijing," *Wall Street Journal* (http://online.wsj.com), May 20, 2014.

Opponents of the United States becoming a party to UNCLOS argue or might argue one or more of the following:

- China's ability to cite international law (including UNCLOS) in defending its position on whether coastal states have a right to regulate foreign military activities in their EEZs[104] shows that UNCLOS does not adequately protect U.S. interests relating to navigational rights in EEZs; the United States should not help lock this inadequate description of navigational rights into permanent international law by becoming a party to the treaty.

- The United States becoming a party to the treaty would do little to help resolve maritime territorial disputes in the SCS and ECS, in part because China's maritime territorial claims, such as those depicted in the map of the nine-dash line, predate and go well beyond what is allowed under the treaty and appear rooted in arguments that are outside the treaty.

- The United States can adequately support the ASEAN countries and Japan in matters relating to maritime territorial disputes in the SCS and ECS in other ways, without becoming a party to the treaty.

- The United States can continue to defend its positions on navigational rights on the high seas by citing customary international law, by demonstrating those rights with U.S. naval deployments (including those conducted under the FON program), and by having allies and partners defend the U.S. position on the EEZ issue at meetings of UNCLOS parties.

Legislative Activity in 113th Congress

H.R. 4435/S. 2410 (FY2015 National Defense Authorization Act)

House

Section 1232 of H.R. 4435 as reported by the House Armed Services Committee (H.Rept. 113-446 of May 13, 2014) states:

> SEC. 1232. MODIFICATIONS TO ANNUAL REPORT ON MILITARY AND SECURITY DEVELOPMENTS INVOLVING THE PEOPLE'S REPUBLIC OF CHINA.
>
> (a) Matters To Be Included- Subsection (b) of section 1202 of the National Defense Authorization Act for Fiscal Year 2000 (P.L. 106-65; 113 Stat. 781; 10 U.S.C. 113 note) is amended—
>
> (1) by redesignating paragraphs (10) through (20) as paragraphs (11) through (21), respectively; and
>
> (2) by inserting after paragraph (9) the following:

---

[104] For a discussion of China's legal justifications for its position on the EEZ issue, see, for example, Peter Dutton, "Three Dispute and Three Objectives," *Naval War College Review*, Autumn 2011: 54-55.

`(10) The developments in maritime law enforcement capabilities and organization of the People's Republic of China, focusing on activities in contested maritime areas in the South China Sea and East China Sea. Such analyses shall include an assessment of the nature of China's maritime law enforcement activities directed against United States allies and partners. Such maritime activities shall include activities originating or suspect of originating from China and shall include government and nongovernment activities that are believed to be sanctioned or supported by the Chinese government.'.

(b) Effective Date- The amendments made by this section take effect on the date of the enactment of this Act and apply with respect to reports required to be submitted under subsection (a) of section 1202 of the National Defense Authorization Act for Fiscal Year 2000, as so amended, on or after that date.

Section 1238 of H.R. 4435 as reported states:

SEC. 1238. SENSE OF CONGRESS REAFFIRMING SECURITY COMMITMENT TO JAPAN.

It is the sense of Congress that—

(1) the United States highly values its alliance with the Government of Japan as a cornerstone of peace and security in the region, based on shared values of democracy, the rule of law, free and open markets, and respect for human rights in order to promote peace, security, stability, and economic prosperity in the Asia-Pacific region;

(2) the United States welcomes Japan's determination to contribute more proactively to regional and global peace and security;

(3) the United States supports recent increases in Japanese defense funding, adoption of a National Security Strategy, formation of security institutions such as the Japanese National Security Council, and other moves that will enable Japan to bear even greater alliance responsibilities;

(4) the United States and Japan should continue to improve joint interoperability and collaborate on developing future capabilities with which to maintain regional stability in an increasingly uncertain security environment;

(5) the United States and Japan should continue efforts to strengthen regional multilateral institutions that promote economic and security cooperation based on internationally accepted rules and norms;

(6) the United States acknowledges that the Senkaku Islands are under the administration of Japan and opposes any unilateral actions that would seek to undermine such administration and remains committed under the Treaty of Mutual Cooperation and Security to respond to any armed attack in the territories under the administration of Japan; and

(7) the United States reaffirms its commitment to the Government of Japan under Article V of the Treaty of Mutual Cooperation and Security that `[e]ach Party recognizes that an armed attack against either Party in the territories under the administration of Japan would be dangerous to its own peace and safety and declares that it would act to meet the common danger in accordance with its constitutional provisions and processes'.

Senate

Section 1245 of S. 2410 as reported by the Senate Armed Services Committee (S.Rept. 113-176 of June 2, 2014) states:

> SEC. 1245. REPORT ON MARITIME SECURITY STRATEGY AND ANNUAL BRIEFING ON MILITARY TO MILITARY ENGAGEMENT WITH THE PEOPLE'S REPUBLIC OF CHINA.
>
> (a) Report Required-
>
> (1) IN GENERAL- Not later than 90 days after the date of the enactment of this Act, the President shall submit to the congressional defense committees a report that outlines the strategy of the Department of Defense with regard to maritime security in the South China Sea and the East China Sea that seeks to balance the interests of the United States, the People's Republic of China, and other countries in the region.
>
> (2) ELEMENTS- The report required by paragraph (1) shall outline the strategy described in that paragraph and include the following:
>
> (A) A description of any current or planned bilateral or regional maritime capacity building initiatives in the South China Sea and the East China Sea region.
>
> (B) An assessment of anti-access and area denial capabilities of the People's Republic of China in the region, including weapons and technologies, and their impact on United States maritime strategy in the region.
>
> (C) An assessment of how the actions of the People's Republic of China in the South China Sea and the East China Sea have changed the status quo with regard to competing territorial and maritime claims in those seas.
>
> (D) A detailed analysis and assessment of the manner in which military to military engagements between the United States and the People's Republic of China facilitates a reduction in potential miscalculation and tension in the South China Sea and the East China Sea, including a specific description of the effect of such engagements on particular incidents or interactions involving the People's Republic of China in those seas.
>
> (E) A description of the naval modernization efforts of the People's Republic of China, including both defense and law enforcement capabilities and the implications of such efforts for United States maritime strategy in the region.
>
> (3) FORM- The report required by paragraph (1) shall be submitted in unclassified form, but may include a classified annex.
>
> (b) Briefings- Not later than May 15 each year, the Secretary of Defense shall provide the congressional defense committees a briefing (in classified form, if appropriate) on the following:
>
> (1) An outline in detail of all of the planned and potential military to military engagements between the United States and the People's Republic of China during the fiscal year beginning in the year of such briefing, including the objectives of such engagements.
>
> (2) An assessment of the military to military engagements between the United States and the People's Republic of China during the fiscal year ending in the year preceding such briefing,

and during the first fiscal half year of the fiscal year of such briefing, including an assessment of the success of such engagements in meeting the objectives of the Commander of the United States Pacific Command for such engagements.

H.R. 1960 (FY2014 National Defense Authorization Act)

Section 1257 of H.R. 1960 as reported by the House Armed Services Committee (H.Rept. 113-102 of June 7, 2013) states:

SEC. 1257. SENSE OF CONGRESS ON MILITARY CAPABILITIES OF THE PEOPLE'S REPUBLIC OF CHINA.

Congress—

(1) notes the People's Republic of China (PRC) continues to rapidly modernize and expand its military capabilities across the land, sea, air, space, and cyberspace domains;

(2) is concerned by the rate and scope of PRC military developments, including its military-focused cyber espionage, which indicate a desire to constrain or prevent the peaceful activities of the United States and its allies in the Western Pacific;

(3) concurs with Admiral Samuel Locklear, commander of U.S. Pacific Command, that `China's rapid development of advanced military capabilities, combined with its unclear intentions, certainly raises strategic and security concerns for the U.S and the region';

(4) notes the United States remains committed to a robust forward military-presence in the Asia-Pacific and will continue to vigorously support mutual defense arrangements with treaty allies while also building deeper relationships with other strategic partners in the region; and

(5) urges the Government of the PRC to work peacefully to resolve existing territorial disputes and to adopt a maritime code of conduct with relevant parties to guide all forms of maritime interaction and communications in the Asia-Pacific.

This section was not included in the final version of the FY2014 National Defense Authorization Act (H.R. 3304/P.L. 113-66 of December 26, 2013.). The explanatory statement for H.R. 3304 states:

Sense of Congress on military capabilities of the People's Republic of China

The House bill contained a provision (sec. 1257) that would express certain findings and the sense of Congress regarding the military developments of the People's Republic of China.

The Senate committee-reported bill contained no similar provision.

The agreement does not include the provision.

We reaffirm our interest in the Asia-Pacific region and the implementation of the rebalance to that region, as described in the Defense Strategic Guidance, dated January 2012. We encourage the Secretary of Defense to continue engaging with the congressional defense committees to facilitate the successful implementation of the strategic rebalance and to continue to support the national security interests of the United States and its allies and partners in the Asia-Pacific region. (Page 223)

H.R. 4495

H.R. 4495, introduced on April 28, 2014, is a bill to "strengthen the United States commitment to the security and stability of the Asia-Pacific region, and for other purposes." The table of contents of the bill, as presented in Section 1 of the bill, are as follows:

SECTION 1. SHORT TITLE; TABLE OF CONTENTS.

(a) Short Title- This Act may be cited as the `Asia-Pacific Region Priority Act'.

(b) Table of Contents- The table of contents for this Act is as follows:

Sec. 1. Short title; table of contents.

Sec. 2. Sense of Congress.

Sec. 3. Congressional defense committees.

TITLE I—MATTERS RELATING TO THE DEPARTMENT OF DEFENSE

Sec. 101. Report on Department of Defense munitions strategy for United States Pacific Command.

Sec. 102. Establishment of Department of Defense unmanned systems office.

Sec. 103. Independent assessment on countering anti-access and area-denial capabilities in the Asia-Pacific region.

Sec. 104. Assessment of the maritime balance of forces in the Asia-Pacific region.

Sec. 105. Missile defense cooperation.

Sec. 106. Department of Defense Space Security and Defense Program.

Sec. 107. Space situational awareness.

Sec. 108. Sense of Congress on access to training ranges within United States Pacific Command area of responsibility.

Sec. 109. Sense of Congress on Pohakuloa Training Area in Hawaii.

Sec. 110. Special easement acquisition authority, Pacific Missile Range Facility, Barking Sands, Kauai, Hawaii.

TITLE II—MATTERS RELATING TO FOREIGN NATIONS

Sec. 201. Statement of policy on maritime disputes in the Asia-Pacific region.

Sec. 202. Sense of Congress reaffirming security commitment to Japan.

Sec. 203. Report on opportunities to strengthen relationship between the United States and the Republic of Korea.

Sec. 204. Maritime capabilities of Taiwan and its contribution to regional peace and stability.

Sec. 205. Modifications to annual report on military and security developments involving the People's Republic of China.

H.R. 772

H.R. 772 was introduced in the House on February 15, 2013. The text of H.R. 772 as introduced is as follows:

A BILL

To promote peaceful and collaborative resolution of the South China Sea dispute.

Be it enacted by the Senate and House of Representatives of the United States of America in Congress assembled,

SECTION 1. FINDINGS.

Congress finds the following:

(1) The South China Sea contains vital commercial shipping lanes and points of access between the Indian Ocean and Pacific Ocean, providing a maritime lifeline to India, Singapore, Malaysia, Indonesia, the Philippines, Vietnam, Brunei, Taiwan, Japan, and the Korean peninsula.

(2) China, Vietnam, the Philippines, Taiwan, Malaysia, and Brunei have disputed territorial claims over the Spratly Islands, and China, Taiwan, and Vietnam have disputed territorial claims over the Paracel Islands.

(3) In 2009, the Government of the People's Republic of China submitted to the United Nations a map with the 9-dotted line (also known as the Cow Tongue line) which raised questions about whether China officially claims most of the 1,423,000 square miles of the South China Sea, more than any other nation involved in these territorial disputes.

(4) In November 2012, China began to include a map of its territorial claims inside its passports, despite the protests of its neighbors, including Vietnam and the Philippines.

(5) Although not a party to these disputes, the United States has a national economic and security interest in maintaining peace, stability, and prosperity in East Asia and Southeast Asia, and ensuring that no party threatens or uses force or coercion unilaterally to assert maritime territorial claims in East Asia and Southeast Asia, including in the South China Sea, the East China Sea, or the Yellow Sea.

(6) The Association of Southeast Asian Nations (ASEAN) has promoted multilateral talks in disputed areas without settling the issue of sovereignty.

(7) In 2002, ASEAN and China signed a Declaration on the Conduct of Parties in the South China Sea.

(8) That declaration committed all parties to those territorial disputes to 'reaffirm their respect for and commitment to the freedom of navigation in and over flight above the South China Sea as provided for by the universally recognized principles of international law', and

to 'resolve their territorial and jurisdictional disputes by peaceful means, without resorting to the threat or use of force'.

(9) In July and November of 2010, the United States and our Republic of Korea allies conducted joint naval exercises in the Yellow Sea in international waters, as well as Republic of Korea territorial waters, in the vicinity of the site of the March 2010 North Korean attack on the South Korean military vessel Cheonan, these exercises drew objections from Beijing over foreign operations in the Yellow Sea.

(10) In September 2010, tensions were raised in the East China Sea near the Senkaku (Diaoyutai) Islands, a territory under the legal administration of Japan, when a Chinese fishing vessel deliberately rammed Japanese Coast Guard patrol boats.

(11) On February 25, 2011, a frigate from China's navy fired shots at 3 fishing boats from the Philippines.

(12) On March 2, 2011, the Government of the Philippines reported that two patrol boats from China attempted to ram one of its surveillance ships.

(13) On May 26, 2011, a maritime security vessel from China cut the cables of an exploration ship from Vietnam, the Binh Minh, in the South China Sea in waters near Cam Ranh Bay in the exclusive economic zone of Vietnam.

(14) On May 31, 2011, three Chinese military vessels used guns to threaten the crews of four Vietnamese fishing boats while they were fishing in the waters of the Truong Sa (Spratly) archipelago.

(15) On June 3, 2011, Vietnam's Foreign Ministry released a statement that 'Vietnam is resolutely opposed to these acts by China that seriously violated the sovereign and jurisdiction rights of Viet Nam to its continental shelf and Exclusive Economic Zone (EEZ)'.

(16) On June 9, 2011, three vessels from China, including one fishing vessel and two maritime security vessels, ran into and disabled the cables of another exploration ship from Vietnam, the Viking 2, in the exclusive economic zone of Vietnam.

(17) The actions of the Government of the People's Republic of China in the South China Sea have also affected United States military and maritime vessels and aircraft transiting through international air space and waters, including the collision of a Chinese fighter plane with a United States surveillance plane in 2001, the harassment of the USNS Victorious and the USNS Impeccable in March 2009, and the collision of a Chinese submarine with the sonar cable of the USS John McCain in June 2009.

(18) On July 23, 2010, former Secretary of State Hillary Rodham Clinton stated at the ASEAN Regional Forum that the United States, like every nation, has a national interest in freedom of navigation, open access to Asia's maritime commons, respect for international law, and unimpeded commerce in the South China Sea.

(19) On June 23, 2011, the United States stated that it was ready to provide hardware to modernize the military of the Philippines.

(20) The United States and the Philippines conducted combined naval exercises in the Sulu Sea, near the South China Sea, from June 28 to July 8, 2011.

(21) On July 22, 2011, an Indian naval vessel, sailing about 45 nautical miles off the coast of Vietnam, was warned by a Chinese naval vessel that it was allegedly violating Chinese territorial waters.

(22) In June 2012, China's cabinet, the State Council, approved the establishment of the city of Sansha to oversee the areas claimed by China in the South China Sea.

(23) In July 2012, Chinese military authorities announced that they had established a corresponding Sansha garrison in the new prefecture.

(24) On June 23, 2012, the China National Offshore Oil Corporation invited bids for oil exploration in areas within 200 nautical miles of the continental shelf and within the exclusive economic zone of Vietnam.

(25) Since July 2012, Chinese patrol ships have been spotted near the disputed Senkaku (Diaoyutai) Islands in the East China Sea.

(26) At the July 2012 ASEAN Regional Forum, former Secretary of State Clinton said, `We believe the nations of the region should work collaboratively and diplomatically to resolve disputes without coercion, without intimidation, without threats, and without the use of force'.

(27) In November 2012, a regulation was approved by the Hainan People's Congress authorizing Chinese maritime police to `board, search' and even `take over' ships determined to be `illegally entering' South China Sea waters unilaterally claimed by Beijing.

(28) At a meeting with the Japanese Foreign Minister on January 18, 2013, former Secretary of State Clinton stated that `although the United States does not take a position on the ultimate sovereignty of the (Senkaku) islands, we acknowledge they are under the administration of Japan', adding that `We oppose any unilateral actions that would seek to undermine Japanese administration, and we urge all parties to take steps to prevent incidents and manage disagreements through peaceful means'.

(29) On August 3, 2012, a Department of State spokesperson expressed concern over `China's upgrading of the administrative level of Sansha City and the establishment of a new military garrison there', expressed encouragement for ASEAN and China `to make meaningful progress toward finalizing a comprehensive Code of Conduct', and called upon claimants to `explore every diplomatic or other peaceful avenue for resolution, including the use of arbitration or other international legal mechanisms as needed'.

SEC. 2. SENSE OF CONGRESS.

It is the sense of Congress that, in light of the congressional finding described above, the Secretary of State should—

(1) reaffirm the strong support of the United States for the peaceful resolution of maritime territorial disputes in the South China Sea, the Taiwan Strait, the East China Sea, and the Yellow Sea and pledge continued efforts to facilitate a collaborative, peaceful process to resolve these disputes;

(2) condemn the use of threats or force by naval, maritime security, and fishing vessels from China in the South China Sea and the East China Sea as well as the use of force by North Korea in the Yellow Sea that would escalate tensions or result in miscalculations;

(3) note that overt threats and gun boat diplomacy are not constructive means for settling these outstanding maritime disputes;

(4) welcome the diplomatic efforts of Association of Southeast Asian Nations (ASEAN) and the United States allies and partners in Japan, the Republic of Korea, Taiwan, the Philippines, and India to amiably and fairly resolve these outstanding disputes; and

(5) support the continuation of operations by the United States Armed Forces in support of freedom of navigation rights in international waters and air space in the South China Sea, the East China Sea, the Taiwan Strait, and the Yellow Sea.

SEC. 3. REPORT ON THE CODE OF CONDUCT FOR THE SOUTH CHINA SEA.

(a) Report- Not later than 180 days after the date of the enactment of this Act, the Secretary of State shall submit to the Committee on Foreign Affairs of the House of Representatives and the Committee on Foreign Relations of the Senate a report on the Code of Conduct and other peaceful measures for resolution of the territorial disputes in the South China Sea.

(b) Form- The report required under subsection (a) shall be submitted in unclassified form, but may contain a classified annex if necessary.

S.Res. 412

S.Res. 412 was introduced on April 7, 2014. On May 20, 2014, it was reported by Senator Menendez with amendments and with an amended preamble, and without a written report. The text of the resolution as reported is as follows:

RESOLUTION

Reaffirming the strong support of the United States Government for freedom of navigation and other internationally lawful uses of sea and airspace in the Asia-Pacific region, and for the peaceful diplomatic resolution of outstanding territorial and maritime claims and disputes.

Whereas Asia-Pacific's maritime domains, which include both the sea and airspace above the domains, are critical to the region's prosperity, stability, and security, including global commerce;

Whereas the United States is a longstanding Asia-Pacific power and has a national interest in maintaining freedom of operations in international waters and airspace both in the Asia-Pacific region and around the world;

Whereas, for over 60 years, the United States Government, alongside United States allies and partners, has played an instrumental role in maintaining stability in the Asia-Pacific, including safeguarding the prosperity and economic growth and development of the Asia-Pacific region;

Whereas the United States, from the earliest days of the Republic, has had a deep and abiding national security interest in freedom of navigation, freedom of the seas, respect for international law, and unimpeded lawful commerce, including in the East China and South China Seas;

Whereas the United States alliance relationships in the region, including with Japan, Korea, Australia, the Philippines, and Thailand, are at the heart of United States policy and engagement in the Asia-Pacific region, and share a common approach to supporting the maintenance of peace and stability, freedom of navigation, and other internationally lawful uses of sea and airspace in the Asia-Pacific region;

Whereas territorial and maritime claims must be derived from land features and otherwise comport with international law;

Whereas the United States Government has a clear interest in encouraging and supporting the nations of the region to work collaboratively and diplomatically to resolve disputes and is firmly opposed to coercion, intimidation, threats, or the use of force;

Whereas the South China Sea contains great natural resources, and their stewardship and responsible use offers immense potential benefit for generations to come;

Whereas the United States is not a claimant party in either the East China or South China Seas, but does have an interest in the peaceful diplomatic resolution of disputed claims in accordance with international law, in freedom of operations, and in the free-flow of commerce free of coercion, intimidation, or the use of force;

Whereas the United States supports the obligation of all members of the United Nations to seek to resolve disputes by peaceful means;

Whereas freedom of navigation and other lawful uses of sea and airspace in the Asia-Pacific region are embodied in international law, not granted by certain states to others;

Whereas, on November 23, 2013, the People's Republic of China unilaterally and without prior consultations with the United States, Japan, the Republic of Korea or other nations of the Asia-Pacific region, declared an Air Defense Identification Zone (ADIZ) in the East China Sea, also announcing that all aircraft entering the PRC's self-declared ADIZ, even if they do not intend to enter Chinese territorial airspace, would have to submit flight plans, maintain radio contact, and follow directions from the Chinese Ministry of National Defense or face `emergency defensive measures';

Whereas the `rules of engagement' declared by China, including the `emergency defensive measures', are in violation of the concept of `due regard for the safety of civil aviation' under the Chicago Convention of the International Civil Aviation Organization's Chicago Convention and thereby are a departure from accepted practice;

Whereas the Chicago Convention of the International Civil Aviation Organization distinguishes between civilian aircraft and state aircraft and provides for the specific obligations of state parties, consistent with customary law, to `refrain from resorting to the use of weapons against civil aircraft in flight and . . . in case of interception, the lives of persons on board and the safety of aircraft must not be endangered';

Whereas international civil aviation is regulated by international agreements, including standards and regulations set by ICAO for aviation safety, security, efficiency and regularity, as well as for aviation environmental protection;

Whereas, in accordance with the norm of airborne innocent passage, the United States does not recognize the right of a coastal nation to apply its ADIZ procedures to foreign state aircraft not intending to enter national airspace nor does the United States apply its ADIZ procedures to foreign state aircraft not intending to enter United States airspace;

Whereas the United States Government expressed profound concerns with China's unilateral, provocative, dangerous, and destabilizing declaration of such a zone, including the potential for misunderstandings and miscalculations by aircraft operating lawfully in international airspace;

Whereas the People's Republic of China's declaration of an ADIZ in the East China Sea will not alter how the United States Government conducts operations in the region or the unwavering United States commitment to peace, security and stability in the Asia-Pacific region;

Whereas the Government of Japan expressed deep concern about the People's Republic of China's declaration of such a zone, regarding it as an effort to unduly infringe upon the freedom of flight in international airspace and to change the status quo that could escalate tensions and potentially cause unintentional consequences in the East China Sea;

Whereas the Government of the Republic of Korea has expressed concern over China's declared ADIZ, and on December 9, 2013, announced an adjustment to its longstanding Air Defense Identification Zone, which does not encompass territory administered by another country, and did so only after undertaking a deliberate process of consultations with the United States, Japan, and China;

Whereas the Government of the Philippines has stressed that China's declared ADIZ seeks to transfer an entire air zone into Chinese domestic airspace, infringes on freedom of flight in international airspace, and compromises the safety of civil aviation and the national security of affected states, and has called on China to ensure that its actions do not jeopardize regional security and stability;

Whereas, on November 26, 2013, the Government of Australia made clear in a statement its opposition to any coercive or unilateral actions to change the status quo in the East China Sea;

Whereas, on March 10, 2014, the United States Government and the Government of Japan jointly submitted a letter to the ICAO Secretariat regarding the issue of freedom of overflight by civil aircraft in international airspace and the effective management of civil air traffic within allocated Flight Information Regions (FIR);

Whereas Indonesia Foreign Minister Marty Natalegawa, in a hearing before the Committee on Defense and Foreign Affairs on February 18, 2014, stated, `We have firmly told China we will not accept a similar [Air Defense Identification] Zone if it is adopted in the South China Sea. And the signal we have received thus far is, China does not plan to adopt a similar Zone in the South China Sea.';

Whereas over half the world's merchant tonnage flows through the South China Sea, and over 15,000,000 barrels of oil per day transit the Strait of Malacca, fueling economic growth and prosperity throughout the Asia-Pacific region;

Whereas the increasing frequency and assertiveness of patrols and competing regulations over disputed territory and maritime areas and airspace in the South China Sea and the East China Sea are raising tensions and increasing the risk of confrontation;

Whereas the Association of Southeast Asian Nations (ASEAN) has promoted multilateral talks on disputed areas without settling the issue of sovereignty, and in 2002 joined with China in signing a Declaration on the Conduct of Parties in the South China Sea that committed all parties to those territorial disputes to `reaffirm their respect for and commitment to the freedom of navigation in and over flight above the South China Sea as provided for by the universally recognized principles of international law' and to `resolve their territorial and jurisdictional disputes by peaceful means, without resorting to the threat or use of force';

Whereas ASEAN and China committed in 2002 to develop an effective Code of Conduct when they adopted the Declaration on the Conduct of Parties in the South China Sea, yet negotiations are irregular and little progress has been made;

Whereas, in recent years, there have been numerous dangerous and destabilizing incidents in waters near the coasts of the Philippines, China, Malaysia, and Vietnam;

Whereas the United States Government is deeply concerned about unilateral actions by any claimant seeking to change the status quo through the use of coercion, intimidation, or military force, including the continued restrictions on access to Scarborough Reef and pressure on long-standing Philippine presence at the Second Thomas Shoal by the People's Republic of China; actions by any state to prevent any other state from exercising its sovereign rights to the resources of the exclusive economic zone (EEZ) and continental shelf by making claims to those areas that have no support in international law; declarations of administrative and military districts in contested areas in the South China Sea; and the imposition of new fishing regulations covering disputed areas, which have raised tensions in the region;

Whereas international law is important to safeguard the rights and freedoms of all states in the Asia-Pacific region, and the lack of clarity in accordance with international law by claimants with regard to their South China Sea claims can create uncertainty, insecurity, and instability;

Whereas the United States Government opposes the use of intimidation, coercion, or force to assert a territorial claim in the South China Sea;

Whereas claims in the South China Sea must accord with international law, and those that are not derived from land features are fundamentally flawed;

Whereas ASEAN issued Six-Point Principles on the South China Sea on July 20, 2012, whereby ASEAN's Foreign Ministers reiterated and reaffirmed `the commitment of ASEAN Member States to: . . . 1. the full implementation of the Declaration on the Conduct of Parties in the South China Sea (2002); . . . 2. the Guidelines for the Implementation of the Declaration on the Conduct of Parties in the South China Sea (2011); . . . 3. the early conclusion of a Regional Code of Conduct in the South China Sea; . . . 4. the full respect of the universally recognized principles of International Law, including the 1982 United Nations Convention on the Law of the Sea (UNCLOS); . . . 5. the continued exercise of self-restraint and non-use of force by all parties; and . . . 6. the peaceful resolution of disputes, in accordance with universally recognized principles of International Law, including the 1982 United Nations Convention on the Law of the Sea (UNCLOS).';

Whereas, in 2013, the Republic of the Philippines properly exercised its rights to peaceful settlement mechanisms with the filing of arbitration case under Article 287 and Annex VII of the Convention on the Law of the Sea in order to achieve a peaceful and durable solution to the dispute, and the United States hopes that all parties in any dispute ultimately abide by the rulings of internationally recognized dispute-settlement bodies;

Whereas China and Japan are the world's second and third largest economies, and have a shared interest in preserving stable maritime domains to continue to support economic growth;

Whereas there has been an unprecedented increase in dangerous activities by Chinese maritime agencies in areas near the Senkaku islands, including between 6 and 25 ships of the Government of China intruding into the Japanese territorial sea each month since September 2012, between 26 and 124 ships entering the `contiguous zone' in the same time period, and 9 ships intruding into the territorial sea and 33 ships entering in the contiguous zone in February 2014;

Whereas, although the United States Government does not take a position on the ultimate sovereignty of the Senkaku Islands, the United States Government acknowledges that they are under the administration of Japan and opposes any unilateral actions that would seek to undermine such administration;

Whereas the United States Senate has previously affirmed that the unilateral actions of a third party will not affect the United States acknowledgment of the administration of Japan over the Senkaku Islands;

Whereas the United States remains committed under the Treaty of Mutual Cooperation and Security to respond to any armed attack in the territories under the administration of Japan, has urged all parties to take steps to prevent incidents and manage disagreements through peaceful means, and commends the Government of Japan for its restrained approach in this regard;

Whereas both the United States and the People's Republic of China are parties to and are obligated to observe the rules of the Convention on the International Regulations for Preventing Collisions at Sea, done at London October 12, 1972 (COLREGs);

Whereas, on December 5, 2013, the USS Cowpens was lawfully operating in international waters in the South China Sea when a People's Liberation Army Navy vessel reportedly crossed its bow at a distance of less than 500 yards and stopped in the water, forcing the USS Cowpens to take evasive action to avoid a collision;

Whereas the reported actions taken by the People's Liberation Army Navy vessel in the USS Cowpens' incident, as publicly reported, appear contrary to the international legal obligations of the People's Republic of China under COLREGs;

Whereas, on May 1, 2014, the People's Republic of China's state-owned energy company, CNOOC, placed its deepwater semi-submersible drilling rig Hai Yang Shi You 981 (HD-981), accompanied by over 25 Chinese ships, in Block 143, 120 nautical miles off Vietnam's coastline;

Whereas, from May 1 to May 9, 2014, the number of Chinese vessels escorting HD-981 increased to more than 80, including seven military ships, which aggressively patrolled and intimidated Vietnamese Coast Guard ships in violation of COLREGS, reportedly intentionally rammed multiple Vietnamese vessels, and used helicopters and water cannons to obstruct others;

Whereas, on May 5, 2014, vessels from the Maritime Safety Administration of China (MSAC) established an exclusion zone with a radius of three nautical miles around HD-981, which undermines maritime safety in the area and is in violation of universally recognized principles of International Law, including the 1982 United Nations Convention on the Law of the Sea (UNCLOS);

Whereas China's territorial claims and associated maritime actions in support of the drilling activity that HD-981 commenced on May 1, 2014, have not been clarified under international law, including as defined by the 1982 United Nations Convention on the Law of the Sea, constitute a unilateral attempt to change the status quo by force, and appear to be in violation of the 2002 Declaration on the Conduct of Parties in the South China Sea;

Whereas, on January 19, 1998, the United States and People's Republic of China signed the Military Maritime Consultative Agreement, creating a mechanism for consultation and coordination on operational safety issues in the maritime domain between the United States and the People's Republic of China;

Whereas the Western Pacific Naval Symposium, inaugurated in 1988 and comprising the navies of Australia, Brunei, Cambodia, Canada, Chile, France, Indonesia, Japan, Malaysia, New Zealand, Papua New Guinea, the People's Republic of China, the Philippines, the Republic of Korea, the Russian Federation, Singapore, Thailand, Tonga, the United States, and Vietnam, whose countries all border the Pacific Ocean region, provides a forum where leaders of regional navies can meet to discuss cooperative initiatives, discuss regional and global maritime issues, and undertake exercises to strengthen norms and practices that contribute to operational safety, including protocols for unexpected encounters at sea, common ways of communication, common ways of operating, and common ways of engagement;

Whereas, Japan and the People's Republic of China sought to negotiate a Maritime Communications Mechanism between the defense authorities and a Maritime Search and Rescue Agreement and agreed in principle to these agreements to address operational safety on the maritime domains but failed to sign them;

Whereas the Changi Command and Control Center in Singapore provides a platform for all the countries of the Western Pacific to share information on what kind of contact at sea and to provide a common operational picture for the region;

Whereas 2014 commemorates the 35th anniversary of normalization of diplomatic relations between the United States and the People's Republic of China, and the United States welcomes the development of a peaceful and prosperous China that becomes a responsible international stakeholder, the government of which respects international norms, international laws, international institutions, and international rules; enhances security and peace; and seeks to advance relations between the United States and China; and

Whereas ASEAN plays an important role, in partnership with others in the regional and international community, in addressing maritime security issues in the Asia-Pacific region and the Indian Ocean, including open access to the maritime domain of Asia; Now, therefore, be it

Resolved,

SECTION 1. SENSE OF THE SENATE.

The Senate--

(1) condemns coercive and threatening actions or the use of force to impede freedom of operations in international airspace by military or civilian aircraft, to alter the status quo or to destabilize the Asia-Pacific region;

(2) urges the Government of the People's Republic of China to refrain from implementing the declared East China Sea Air Defense Identification Zone (ADIZ), which is contrary to freedom of overflight in international airspace, and to refrain from taking similar provocative actions elsewhere in the Asia-Pacific region [Struck out->] ; and [<-Struck out] ;

(3) commends the Governments of Japan and of the Republic of Korea for their restraint, and commends the Government of the Republic of Korea for engaging in a deliberate process of consultations with the United States, Japan and China prior to announcing its adjustment of its Air Defense Identification Zone on December 9, 2013, and for its commitment to implement this adjusted Air Defense Identification Zone (ADIZ) in a manner consistent with international practice and respect for the freedom of overflight and other internationally lawful uses of international airspace [Struck out->] . [<-Struck out] ; and

(4) calls on the Government of the People's Republic of China to withdraw its HD-981 drilling rig and associated maritime forces from their current positions, to refrain from maritime maneuvers contrary to COLREGS, and to return immediately to the status quo as it existed before May 1, 2014.

SEC. 2. STATEMENT OF POLICY.

It is the policy of the United States to--

(1) reaffirm its unwavering commitment and support for allies and partners in the Asia-Pacific region, including longstanding United States policy regarding Article V of the United States-Philippines Mutual Defense Treaty and that Article V of the United States-Japan Mutual Defense Treaty applies to the Japanese-administered Senkaku Islands;

(2) oppose claims that impinge on the rights, freedoms, and lawful use of the sea that belong to all nations;

(3) urge all parties to refrain from engaging in destabilizing activities, including illegal occupation or efforts to unlawfully assert administration over disputed claims;

(4) ensure that disputes are managed without intimidation, coercion, or force;

(5) call on all claimants to clarify or adjust claims in accordance with international law;

(6) support efforts by ASEAN and the People's Republic of China to develop an effective Code of Conduct, including the `early harvest' of agreed-upon elements in the Code of Conduct that can be implemented immediately;

(7) reaffirm that an existing body of international rules and guidelines, including the International Regulations for Preventing Collisions at Sea, done at London October 12, 1972 (COLREGs), is sufficient to ensure the safety of navigation between the United States Armed Forces and the forces of other countries, including the People's Republic of China;

(8) support the development of regional institutions and bodies, including the ASEAN Regional Forum, the ASEAN Defense Minister's Meeting Plus, the East Asia Summit, and the expanded ASEAN Maritime Forum, to build practical cooperation in the region and reinforce the role of international law;

(9) encourage the adoption of mechanisms such as hotlines or emergency procedures for preventing incidents in sensitive areas, managing them if they occur, and preventing disputes from escalating;

(10) fully support the rights of claimants to exercise rights they may have to avail themselves of peaceful dispute settlement mechanisms;

(11) encourage claimants not to undertake new unilateral attempts to change the status quo since the signing of the 2002 Declaration of Conduct, including not asserting administrative measures or controls in disputed areas in the South China Sea;

(12) encourage the deepening of partnerships with other countries in the region for maritime domain awareness and capacity building, as well as efforts by the United States Government to explore the development of appropriate multilateral mechanisms for a `common operating picture' in the South China Sea that would serve to help countries avoid destabilizing behavior and deter risky and dangerous activities; and

(13) assure the continuity of operations by the United States in the Asia-Pacific region, including, when appropriate, in cooperation with partners and allies, to reaffirm the principle of freedom of operations in international waters and airspace in accordance with established principles and practices of international law.

S.Res. 167 (Agreed to by the Senate)

S.Res. 167 was introduced in the Senate on June 10, 2013, reported without amendment, with a preamble, and without a written report on June 25, 2013, and agreed to by the Senate by unanimous consent without amendment and an amended preamble on July 29, 2013. The text of S.Res. 167 as agreed to by the Senate is as follows:

RESOLUTION

Reaffirming the strong support of the United States for the peaceful resolution of territorial, sovereignty, and jurisdictional disputes in the Asia-Pacific maritime domains.

Whereas the maritime domain of the Asia-Pacific region includes critical sea lines of communication and commerce between the Pacific and Indian oceans;

Whereas the United States has a national interest in freedom of navigation and overflight in the Asia-Pacific maritime domains, as provided for by universally recognized principles of international law;

Whereas the United States has a national interest in the maintenance of peace and stability, open access by all to maritime domains, respect for universally recognized principles of international law, prosperity and economic growth, and unimpeded lawful commerce;

Whereas although the United States does not take a position on competing territorial claims over land features and maritime boundaries, it does have a strong and long-standing interest in the manner in which disputes in the South China Sea are addressed and in the conduct of the parties;

Whereas the United States has a clear interest in encouraging and supporting the nations of the region to work collaboratively and diplomatically to resolve disputes without coercion, without intimidation, without threats, and without the use of force;

Whereas the South China Sea contains great natural resources, and their stewardship and responsible use offers immense potential benefit for generations to come;

Whereas in recent years, there have been numerous dangerous and destabilizing incidents in this region, including Chinese vessels cutting the seismic survey cables of a Vietnamese oil exploration ship in May 2011; Chinese vessels barricading the entrance to the Scarborough

Reef lagoon in April 2012; China issuing an official map that newly defines the contested 'nine-dash line' as China's national border; and, since May 8, 2013, Chinese naval and marine surveillance ships maintaining a regular presence in waters around the Second Thomas Shoal, located approximately 105 nautical miles northwest of the Philippine island of Palawan;

Whereas the Association of Southeast Asian Nations (ASEAN) has promoted multilateral talks on disputed areas without settling the issue of sovereignty, and in 2002 joined with China in signing a Declaration on the Conduct of Parties in the South China Sea that committed all parties to those territorial disputes to 'reaffirm their respect for and commitment to the freedom of navigation in and over flight above the South China Sea as provided for by the universally recognized principles of international law' and to 'resolve their territorial and jurisdictional disputes by peaceful means, without resorting to the threat or use of force';

Whereas Japan and Taiwan reached an agreement on April 10, 2013, to jointly share and administer the fishing resources in their overlapping claimed exclusive economic zones in the East China Sea, an important breakthrough after 17 years of negotiations and a model for other such agreements;

Whereas other incidences of the joint administrations of resources in disputed waters in the South China Sea have de-escalated tensions and promoted economic development, such as Malaysia and Brunei's 2009 agreement to partner on exploring offshore Brunei waters, with drilling in offshore oil and gas fields off Brunei beginning in 2011; and Thailand and Vietnam's agreement to jointly develop areas of the Gulf of Thailand for gas exports, despite ongoing territorial disputes;

Whereas, on June 21, 2013, the Governments of the People's Republic of China and Vietnam announced that they had agreed to set up and use an emergency fishery hotline to inform each other of any detainment involving fishermen or boats within 48 hours, to help quickly resolve disputes and as part of efforts to prevent future incidents from derailing ties, and the Governments of the People's Republic of China and Indonesia on May 2, 2013, agreed to establish a hotline for incidents in their disputed waters;

Whereas the Government of the Republic of the Philippines states that it 'has exhausted almost all political and diplomatic avenues for a peaceful negotiated settlement of its maritime dispute with China' and in his statement of January 23, 2013, Republic of Philippines Secretary of Foreign Affairs Del Rosario stated that therefore 'the Philippines has taken the step of bringing China before the Arbitral Tribunal under Article 287 and Annex VII of the 1982 Convention on the Law of the Sea in order to achieve a peaceful and durable solution to the dispute';

Whereas, in January 2013, a Chinese naval ship allegedly fixed its weapons-targeting radar on Japanese vessels in the vicinity of the Senkaku islands, and, on April 23, 2013, eight Chinese marine surveillance ships entered the 12-nautical-mile territorial zone off the Senkaku Islands, further escalating regional tensions;

Whereas, on May 8, 2013, the Chinese Communist Party's main newspaper, The People's Daily, published an article by several Chinese scholars questioning Japan's sovereignty over Okinawa, where key United States military installations are located which contribute to preserving security and stability in the Asia-Pacific region;

Whereas the Government of the People's Republic of China has recently taken other unilateral steps, including 'improperly drawing' baselines around the Senkaku Islands in September 2102, which the 2013 Annual Report to Congress on Military and Security

Developments Involving the People's Republic of China found to be `inconsistent with international law', and maintaining a continuous military and paramilitary presence around the Senkaku Islands;

Whereas, on April 27, 2013, Chinese Foreign Ministry spokeswoman, Hua Chunying, was quoted as saying, `The Diaoyu Islands are about sovereignty and territorial integrity. Of course it's China's core interest.';

Whereas although the United States does not take a position on the ultimate sovereignty of the Senkaku Islands, the United States Government acknowledges that they are under the administration of Japan and opposes any unilateral actions that would seek to undermine such administration, affirms that the unilateral actions of a third party will not affect the United States acknowledgment of the administration of Japan over the Senkaku Islands, remains committed under the Treaty of Mutual Cooperation and Security to respond to any armed attack in the territories under the administration of Japan, and has urged all parties to take steps to prevent incidents and manage disagreements through peaceful means;

Whereas, on August 3, 2012, a Department of State spokesperson expressed concern over `China's upgrading of the administrative level of Sansha City and the establishment of a new military garrison there,' encouraged ASEAN and China `to make meaningful progress toward finalizing a comprehensive Code of Conduct,' and called upon claimants to `explore every diplomatic or other peaceful avenue for resolution, including the use of arbitration or other international legal mechanisms as needed';

Whereas the United States recognizes the importance of strong, cohesive, and integrated regional institutions, including the East Asia Summit (EAS), ASEAN, and the Asia-Pacific Economic Cooperation (APEC) forum, as foundation for effective regional frameworks to promote peace and security and economic growth, including in the maritime domain, and to ensure that the Asia-Pacific community develops rules-based regional norms which discourage coercion and the use of force;

Whereas the United States welcomes the development of a peaceful and prosperous China, the government of which respects international norms, international laws, international institutions, and international rules; enhances security and peace; and seeks to advance a `new model' of relations between the United States and China;

Whereas ASEAN plays an important role, in partnership with others in the regional and international community, in addressing maritime security issues in the Asia-Pacific region and into the Indian Ocean, including open access to the maritime domain of Asia;

Whereas ASEAN and China announced on June 30, 2013, that official consultations on a Code of Conduct in the South China Sea will commence at the 6th Senior Officials' Meeting and the 9th Joint Working Group on the Implementation of the Declaration of Conduct of the Parties in the SCS, to be held in China in September 2013; Chinese Foreign Minister Wang Yi reaffirmed that China was willing to advance talks on a code of conduct as part of a `continual, gradual and deepening process'; and Secretary of State John F. Kerry, participating in the ASEAN Regional Forum Ministerial Meeting on July 2, 2013, expressed the hope that announcement of official consultations between ASEAN and China would be the beginning of sustained and substantive official engagement between the two on developing the new Code of Conduct; and

Whereas, from June 17-20, 2013, the 10 ASEAN members and their dialogue partners Australia, China, India, Japan, New Zealand, Russia, South Korea, and the United States jointly participated in the First ASEAN Defense Ministers' Meeting Plus Humanitarian Assistance and Disaster Relief (HADR) and Military Medicine (MM) exercise, helping to establish a new pattern of cooperation among the militaries of the Asia-Pacific: Now, therefore, be it

Resolved, That the Senate—

(1) condemns the use of coercion, threats, or force by naval, maritime security, or fishing vessels and military or civilian aircraft in the South China Sea and the East China Sea to assert disputed maritime or territorial claims or alter the status quo;

(2) strongly urges that all parties to maritime and territorial disputes in the region exercise self-restraint in the conduct of activities that would undermine stability or complicate or escalate disputes, including refraining from inhabiting presently uninhabited islands, reefs, shoals, and other features and handle their differences in a constructive manner;

(3) reaffirms the strong support of the United States for the member states of ASEAN and the Government of the People's Republic of China as they seek to develop a code of conduct of parties in the South China Sea, and urges all countries to substantively support ASEAN in its efforts in this regard;

(4) supports collaborative diplomatic processes by all claimants in the South China Sea for resolving outstanding maritime or territorial disputes, in a manner that maintains peace and security, adheres to international law, and protects unimpeded lawful commerce as well as freedom of navigation and overflight, and including through international arbitration, allowing parties to peacefully settle claims and disputes using universally recognized principles of international law;

(5) encourages the deepening of efforts by the United States Government to develop partnerships with other countries in the region for maritime domain awareness and capacity building; and

(6) supports the continuation of operations by the United States Armed Forces in the Western Pacific, including in partnership with the armed forces of other countries in the region, in support of freedom of navigation, the maintenance of peace and stability, and respect for universally recognized principles of international law, including the peaceful resolution of issues of sovereignty and unimpeded lawful commerce.

An August 1, 2013, press report stated:

> China said on Thursday [August 1] it had lodged a formal complaint with the United States after the U.S. Senate passed a resolution expressing concern about Chinese actions in the disputed East and South China Seas....
>
> "The above resolution proposed by a minority of senators took heed of neither history nor facts, unjustifiably blaming China and sending the wrong message," China's Foreign Ministry said in a statement.
>
> "China expresses its strong opposition, and has already made stern representations with the U.S. side. We urge the relevant senators to respect the facts and correct their mistakes in order to avoid further complicating the issue and the regional situation," it added.[105]

---

[105] Ben Blanchard, "China Condemns U.S. Senate Over Sea Dispute," *Reuters.com*, August 1, 2013.

Appendix A. Legislative Activity in 112ᵗʰ Congress

H.R. 4310/S. 3254 (FY2013 National Defense Authorization Act)

Senate

On November 29, 2012, as part of its consideration of the FY2013 National Defense Authorization Act (S. 3254), the Senate agreed by unanimous consent to **S.Amdt. 3275** to S. 3254, which states:

> At the end of subtitle D of title XII, add the following:
>
> SEC. 1246. SENSE OF THE SENATE ON THE SITUATION IN THE SENKAKU ISLANDS.
>
> It is the sense of the Senate that—
>
> (1) the East China Sea is a vital part of the maritime commons of Asia, including critical sea lanes of communication and commerce that benefit all nations of the Asia-Pacific region;
>
> (2) the peaceful settlement of territorial and jurisdictional disputes in the East China Sea requires the exercise of self-restraint by all parties in the conduct of activities that would complicate or escalate disputes and destabilize the region, and differences should be handled in a constructive manner consistent with universally recognized principles of customary international law;
>
> (3) while the United States takes no position on the ultimate sovereignty of the Senkaku islands, the United States acknowledges the administration of Japan over the Senkaku Islands;
>
> (4) The unilateral actions of a third party will not affect the United States' acknowledgement of the administration of Japan over the Senkaku Islands;
>
> (5) the United States has national interests in freedom of navigation, the maintenance of peace and stability, respect for international law, and unimpeded lawful commerce;
>
> (6) the United States supports a collaborative diplomatic process by claimants to resolve territorial disputes without coercion, and opposes efforts at coercion, the threat of use of force, or use of force by any claimant in seeking to resolve sovereignty and territorial issues in the East China Sea;
>
> (7) the United States reaffirms its commitment to the Government of Japan under Article V of the Treaty of Mutual Cooperation and Security that ``[e]ach Party recognizes that an armed attack against either Party in the territories under the administration of Japan would be dangerous to its own peace and safety and declares that it would act to meet the common danger in accordance with its constitutional provisions and processes''.

Conference

Section 1286 of the conference report (H.Rept. 112-705 of December 18, 2012) on H.R. 4310/P.L. 112-239 of January 2, 2013, states:

SEC. 1286. SENSE OF CONGRESS ON THE SITUATION IN THE SENKAKU ISLANDS.

It is the sense of Congress that—

(1) the East China Sea is a vital part of the maritime commons of Asia, including critical sea lanes of communication and commerce that benefit all nations of the Asia-Pacific region;

(2) the peaceful settlement of territorial and jurisdictional disputes in the East China Sea requires the exercise of self-restraint by all parties in the conduct of activities that would complicate or escalate disputes and destabilize the region, and differences should be handled in a constructive manner consistent with universally recognized principles of customary international law;

(3) while the United States takes no position on the ultimate sovereignty of the Senkaku Islands, the United States acknowledges the administration of Japan over the Senkaku Islands;

(4) the unilateral action of a third party will not affect the United States' acknowledgment of the administration of Japan over the Senkaku Islands;

(5) the United States has national interests in freedom of navigation, the maintenance of peace and stability, respect for international law, and unimpeded lawful commerce;

(6) the United States supports a collaborative diplomatic process by claimants to resolve territorial disputes without coercion, and opposes efforts at coercion, the threat of use of force, or use of force by any claimant in seeking to resolve sovereignty and territorial issues in the East China Sea; and

(7) the United States reaffirms its commitment to the Government of Japan under Article V of the Treaty of Mutual Cooperation and Security that "[e]ach Party recognizes that an armed attack against either Party in the territories under the administration of Japan would be dangerous to its own peace and safety and declares that it would act to meet the common danger in accordance with its constitutional provisions and processes".

S.Res. 524 (Agreed to by the Senate)

This resolution, reaffirming the strong support of the United States for the 2002 declaration of conduct of parties in the South China Sea among the member states of ASEAN and the People's Republic of China, and for other purposes, was introduced on July 23, 2012, and agreed to in Senate without amendment and an amended preamble by unanimous consent on August 2, 2012.

S.Res. 217 (Agreed to by the Senate)

This resolution, calling for a peaceful and multilateral resolution to maritime territorial disputes in Southeast Asia, was introduced on June 27, 2011, and considered, and agreed to without amendment and with a preamble by unanimous consent the same day.

H.R. 6313

This bill to promote peaceful and collaborative resolution of maritime territorial disputes in the South China Sea and its environs and other maritime areas adjacent to the East Asian mainland was introduced on August 2, 2012.

H.Res. 352

This resolution, calling for a peaceful and collaborative resolution of maritime territorial disputes in the South China Sea and its environs and other maritime areas adjacent to the East Asian mainland, was introduced on July 15, 2011.

H.Res. 616

This resolution, expressing the sense of the House of Representatives regarding United States relations with the People's Republic of China, was introduced on April 16, 2012. Paragraph 8 of the resolution "encourage[s] the peaceful resolution of maritime territorial disputes in the South China Sea and East China Sea, and support efforts to facilitate a multilateral, peaceful process to resolve these disputes."

Appendix B. 2002 Declaration on Conduct of Parties in South China Sea

The text of the 2002 Declaration on the Conduct of Parties in the South China Sea is as follows:[106]

DECLARATION ON THE CONDUCT OF PARTIES IN THE SOUTH CHINA SEA

The Governments of the Member States of ASEAN and the Government of the People's Republic of China,

REAFFIRMING their determination to consolidate and develop the friendship and cooperation existing between their people and governments with the view to promoting a 21st century-oriented partnership of good neighbourliness and mutual trust;

COGNIZANT of the need to promote a peaceful, friendly and harmonious environment in the South China Sea between ASEAN and China for the enhancement of peace, stability, economic growth and prosperity in the region;

COMMITTED to enhancing the principles and objectives of the 1997 Joint Statement of the Meeting of the Heads of State/Government of the Member States of ASEAN and President of the People's Republic of China;

DESIRING to enhance favourable conditions for a peaceful and durable solution of differences and disputes among countries concerned;

HEREBY DECLARE the following:

1. The Parties reaffirm their commitment to the purposes and principles of the Charter of the United Nations, the 1982 UN Convention on the Law of the Sea, the Treaty of Amity and Cooperation in Southeast Asia, the Five Principles of Peaceful Coexistence, and other universally recognized principles of international law which shall serve as the basic norms governing state-to-state relations;

2. The Parties are committed to exploring ways for building trust and confidence in accordance with the above-mentioned principles and on the basis of equality and mutual respect;

3. The Parties reaffirm their respect for and commitment to the freedom of navigation in and overflight above the South China Sea as provided for by the universally recognized principles of international law, including the 1982 UN Convention on the Law of the Sea;

4. The Parties concerned undertake to resolve their territorial and jurisdictional disputes by peaceful means, without resorting to the threat or use of force, through friendly consultations and negotiations by sovereign states directly concerned, in accordance with universally recognized principles of international law, including the 1982 UN Convention on the Law of the Sea;

---

[106] Text as taken from http://www.aseansec.org/13163 htm.

5. The Parties undertake to exercise self-restraint in the conduct of activities that would complicate or escalate disputes and affect peace and stability including, among others, refraining from action of inhabiting on the presently uninhabited islands, reefs, shoals, cays, and other features and to handle their differences in a constructive manner.

Pending the peaceful settlement of territorial and jurisdictional disputes, the Parties concerned undertake to intensify efforts to seek ways, in the spirit of cooperation and understanding, to build trust and confidence between and among them, including:

a. holding dialogues and exchange of views as appropriate between their defense and military officials;

b. ensuring just and humane treatment of all persons who are either in danger or in distress;

c. notifying, on a voluntary basis, other Parties concerned of any impending joint/combined military exercise; and

d. exchanging, on a voluntary basis, relevant information.

6. Pending a comprehensive and durable settlement of the disputes, the Parties concerned may explore or undertake cooperative activities. These may include the following:

a. marine environmental protection;

b. marine scientific research;

c. safety of navigation and communication at sea;

d. search and rescue operation; and

e. combating transnational crime, including but not limited to trafficking in illicit drugs, piracy and armed robbery at sea, and illegal traffic in arms.

The modalities, scope and locations, in respect of bilateral and multilateral cooperation should be agreed upon by the Parties concerned prior to their actual implementation.

7. The Parties concerned stand ready to continue their consultations and dialogues concerning relevant issues, through modalities to be agreed by them, including regular consultations on the observance of this Declaration, for the purpose of promoting good neighbourliness and transparency, establishing harmony, mutual understanding and cooperation, and facilitating peaceful resolution of disputes among them;

8. The Parties undertake to respect the provisions of this Declaration and take actions consistent therewith;

9. The Parties encourage other countries to respect the principles contained in this Declaration;

10. The Parties concerned reaffirm that the adoption of a code of conduct in the South China Sea would further promote peace and stability in the region and agree to work, on the basis of consensus, towards the eventual attainment of this objective.

Done on the Fourth Day of November in the Year Two Thousand and Two in Phnom Penh, the Kingdom of Cambodia.

Appendix C. February 5, 2014, Testimony of Assistant Secretary of State Daniel Russel

The appendix presents the text of the written statement of Assistant Secretary of State Daniel Russel for a February 5, 2014, hearing before the subcommittee on Asia and the Pacific of the House Foreign Affairs Committee on maritime disputes in East Asia. The text of the statement is as follows:

> Chairman Chabot, Members of the Subcommittee, thank you for the opportunity to testify today on these important issues.
>
> Before I begin, I would also like to take this opportunity to thank you, Chairman Chabot, for your leadership on this issue and for your work to enhance our engagement with the Asia-Pacific region. This Subcommittee has contributed to the rich bipartisan tradition of engaging the Asia-Pacific and advancing U.S. interests there.
>
> The Members of this Subcommittee know well the importance of the Asia-Pacific region to American interests. The broader region boasts over half the world's population, half of the world's GDP, and nearly half of the world's trade, and is home to some of the fastest growing economies in the world. More and more American citizens are now living, working, and studying in this part of the world and people-to-people and family ties between Americans and the peoples of the Asia-Pacific have witnessed tremendous growth. Growing numbers of American companies are investing in and exporting their products and services to rapidly expanding East Asian markets. Asia-Pacific businesses are increasing their profiles in the United States and creating jobs for American workers. And, as the region's economies continue to grow and their interests expand, it becomes increasingly important that the governments and institutions there contribute to upholding and strengthening international law and standards – ranging from human rights to environmental protection to responsible policies on climate change, maritime security, and trade and investment. The effects of what happens in the Asia-Pacific Region will be felt across the globe and have direct implications for America's interests.
>
> It is precisely with this in mind that this administration has for the past five years made sustained engagement in the Asia-Pacific a strategic priority. This is precisely why Secretary Kerry is about to make his fifth visit to Asia in ten months and why he has devoted so much time and effort to meeting, calling and consulting with his Asian counterparts.
>
> We have a strong stake in the continuing economic growth of this region, and we are working to ensure that Americans can fully participate in that growth and share in that prosperity. We are negotiating high-standard trade and investment agreements that will unlock the dynamism of Pacific Rim economies for mutual benefit. We are bolstering regional cooperation on transnational issues through ASEAN and its related institutions. And we are helping countries manage complex environmental issues resulting from rapid development. The common thread running through our strategic rebalancing is a determination to ensure that the Asia-Pacific remains an open, inclusive, and prosperous region guided by widely accepted rules and standards and a respect for international law.
>
> Since the end of the Second World War, a maritime regime based on international law that promotes freedom of navigation and lawful uses of the sea has facilitated Asia's impressive economic growth. The United States, through our our alliances, our security partnerships and our overall military presence and posture, has been instrumental in sustaining that maritime regime and providing the security that has enabled the countries in the region to prosper. As

a maritime nation with global trading networks, the United States has a national interest in freedom of the seas and in unimpeded lawful commerce. From President Thomas Jefferson's actions against the Barbary pirates to President Reagan's decision that the United States will abide by the Law of the Sea Convention's provisions on navigation and other traditional uses of the ocean, American foreign policy has long defended the freedom of the seas. And as we consistently state, we have a national interest in the maintenance of peace and stability; respect for international law; unimpeded lawful commerce; and freedom of navigation and overflight in the East China and South China Seas.

For all these reasons, the tensions arising from maritime and territorial disputes in the Asia-Pacific are of deep concern to us and to our allies. Both the South China and East China Seas are vital thoroughfares for global commerce and energy. Well over half the world's merchant tonnage flows through the South China Sea, and over 15 million barrels of oil per day transited the Strait of Malacca last year, with most of it continuing onward through the East China Sea to three of the world's largest economies—Japan, the Republic of Korea, and China. A simple miscalculation or incident could touch off an escalatory cycle. Confrontations between fishermen and even law enforcement patrols are not unusual in these waters. But the frequency and assertiveness of some countries' patrols are increasing. In addition, the imposition of competing regulations by different countries over disputed territory and associated maritime areas and airspace is raising tensions and increasing the risk of confrontation. We witnessed a tragic incident in May of last year, when a Philippine Coast Guard patrol shot and killed a fisherman from Taiwan. Both sides, to their credit, took steps to prevent an escalation of tensions. But the risk of confrontation could have very serious adverse consequences for all of our economic and security interests.

Accordingly, we have consistently emphasized in our diplomacy in the region as well as in our public messaging the importance of exercising restraint, maintaining open channels of dialogue, lowering rhetoric, behaving safely and responsibly in the sky and at sea, and peacefully resolving territorial and maritime disputes in accordance with international law. We are working to help put in place diplomatic and other structures to lower tensions and manage these disputes peacefully. We have sought to prevent provocative or unilateral actions that disrupt the status quo or jeopardize peace and security. When such actions have occurred, we have spoken out clearly and, where appropriate, taken action. In an effort to build consensus and capabilities in support of these principles, the administration has invested considerably in the development of regional institutions and bodies such as the ASEAN Regional Forum, the ASEAN Defense Ministers Meeting Plus, the East Asia Summit, and the Expanded ASEAN Maritime Forum. These forums, as they continue to develop, play an important role in reinforcing international law and practice and building practical cooperation among member states.

In the South China Sea, we continue to support efforts by ASEAN and China to develop an effective Code of Conduct. Agreement on a Code of Conduct is long overdue and the negotiating process should be accelerated. This is something that China and ASEAN committed to back in 2002 when they adopted their Declaration on the Conduct of Parties in the South China Sea. An effective Code of Conduct would promote a rules-based framework for managing and regulating the behavior of the relevant countries in the South China Sea. A key part of that framework, which we and many others believe should be adopted quickly, is inclusion of mechanisms such as hotlines and emergency procedures for preventing incidents in sensitive areas and managing them when they do occur in ways that prevent disputes from escalating.

And in the East China Sea, we remain concerned about the serious downturn in China-Japan relations. We support Japan's call for diplomacy and crisis management procedures in order to avoid a miscalculation or a dangerous incident. It is important to lower tensions, turn down the rhetoric, and exercise caution and restraint in this sensitive area. China and Japan are the world's second and third largest economies and have a shared interest in a stable environment to facilitate economic growth. Neither these two important countries nor the global economy can afford an unintended clash that neither side seeks or wants. It is imperative that Japan and China use diplomatic means to manage this issue peacefully and set aside matters that can't be resolved at this time.

China's announcement of an Air Defense Identification Zone (ADIZ) over the East China Sea in November was a provocative act and a serious step in the wrong direction. The Senkakus are under the administration of Japan and unilateral attempts to change the status quo raise tensions and do nothing under international law to strengthen territorial claims. The United States neither recognizes nor accepts China's declared East China Sea ADIZ and has no intention of changing how we conduct operations in the region. China should not attempt to implement the ADIZ and should refrain from taking similar actions elsewhere in the region.

Mr. Chairman, we have a deep and long-standing stake in the maintenance of prosperity and stability in the Asia-Pacific and an equally deep and abiding long-term interest in the continuance of freedom of the seas based on the rule of law—one that guarantees, among other things, freedom of navigation and overflight and other internationally lawful uses of the sea related to those freedoms. International law makes clear the legal basis on which states can legitimately assert their rights in the maritime domain or exploit marine resources. By promoting order in the seas, international law is instrumental in safeguarding the rights and freedoms of all countries regardless of size or military strength.

I think it is imperative that we be clear about what we mean when the United States says that we take no position on competing claims to sovereignty over disputed land features in the East China and South China Seas. First of all, we do take a strong position with regard to behavior in connection with any claims: we firmly oppose the use of intimidation, coercion or force to assert a territorial claim. Second, we do take a strong position that maritime claims must accord with customary international law. This means that all maritime claims must be derived from land features and otherwise comport with the international law of the sea. So while we are not siding with one claimant against another, we certainly believe that claims in the South China Sea that are not derived from land features are fundamentally flawed. In support of these principles and in keeping with the longstanding U.S. Freedom of Navigation Program, the United States continues to oppose claims that impinge on the rights, freedoms, and lawful uses of the sea that belong to all nations.

As I just noted, we care deeply about the way countries behave in asserting their claims or managing their disputes. We seek to ensure that territorial and maritime disputes are dealt with peacefully, diplomatically and in accordance with international law. Of course this means making sure that shots aren't fired; but more broadly it means ensuring that these disputes are managed without intimidation, coercion, or force. We have repeatedly made clear that freedom of navigation is reflected in international law, not something to be granted by big states to others. President Obama and Secretary Kerry have made these points forcefully and clearly in their interactions with regional leaders, and I—along with my colleagues in the State Department, Defense Department, the National Security Council and other agencies—have done likewise.

We are also candid with all the claimants when we have concerns regarding their claims or the ways that they pursue them. Deputy Secretary Burns and I were in Beijing earlier this month to hold regular consultations with the Chinese government on Asia-Pacific issues, and we held extensive discussions regarding our concerns. These include continued restrictions on access to Scarborough Reef; pressure on the long-standing Philippine presence at the Second Thomas Shoal; putting hydrocarbon blocks up for bid in an area close to another country's mainland and far away even from the islands that China is claiming; announcing administrative and even military districts in contested areas in the South China Sea; an unprecedented spike in risky activity by China's maritime agencies near the Senkaku Islands; the sudden, uncoordinated and unilateral imposition of regulations over contested airspace in the case of the East China Sea Air Defense Identification Zone; and the recent updating of fishing regulations covering disputed areas in the South China Sea. These actions have raised tensions in the region and concerns about China's objectives in both the South China and the East China Seas.

There is a growing concern that this pattern of behavior in the South China Sea reflects an incremental effort by China to assert control over the area contained in the so-called "nine-dash line," despite the objections of its neighbors and despite the lack of any explanation or apparent basis under international law regarding the scope of the claim itself. China's lack of clarity with regard to its South China Sea claims has created uncertainty, insecurity and instability in the region. It limits the prospect for achieving a mutually agreeable resolution or equitable joint development arrangements among the claimants. I want to reinforce the point that under international law, maritime claims in the South China Sea must be derived from land features. Any use of the "nine dash line" by China to claim maritime rights not based on claimed land features would be inconsistent with international law. The international community would welcome China to clarify or adjust its nine-dash line claim to bring it in accordance with the international law of the sea.

We support serious and sustained diplomacy between the claimants to address overlapping claims in a peaceful, non-coercive way. This can and should include bilateral as well as multilateral diplomatic dialogue among the claimants. But at the same time we fully support the right of claimants to exercise rights they may have to avail themselves of peaceful dispute settlement mechanisms. The Philippines chose to exercise such a right last year with the filing of an arbitration case under the Law of the Sea Convention.

Both legal and diplomatic processes will take time to play out. The effort to reach agreement on a China-ASEAN Code of Conduct has been painfully slow. However, there are important steps that the relevant parties can take in the short term to lower tensions and avoid escalation. One line of effort, as I mentioned earlier, is to put in place practical mechanisms to prevent incidents or manage them when they occur. Another common-sense measure would be for the claimants to agree not to undertake new unilateral attempts to change the status quo, defined as of the date of the signing of the 2002 Declaration of Conduct, that would include agreement not to assert administrative measures or controls in disputed areas. And as I have indicated, all claimants—not only China—should clarify their claims in terms of international law, including the law of the sea.

In the meantime, a strong diplomatic and military presence by the United States, including by strengthening and modernizing our alliances and continuing to build robust strategic partnerships, remains essential to maintain regional stability. This includes our efforts to promote best practices and good cooperation on all aspects of maritime security and bolster maritime domain awareness and our capacity building programs in Southeast Asia. The Administration has also consistently made clear our desire to build a strong and cooperative relationship with China to advance peace and prosperity in the Asia-Pacific, just as we consistently have encouraged all countries in the region to pursue positive relations with China. And this includes working with all countries in the region to strengthen regional institutions like ASEAN and the East Asia Summit as venues where countries can engage in clear dialogue with all involved about principles, values and interests at stake, while developing cooperative activities – like the Expanded ASEAN Seafarers Training initiative we recently launched – to build trust and mechanisms to reduce the chances of incidents.

To conclude, this is an issue of immense importance to the United States, the Asia-Pacific, and the world. And I want to reaffirm here today that the United States will continue to play a central role in underwriting security and stability in the Asia-Pacific.

Mr. Chairman, I thank you for this opportunity to appear before you today to discuss this important issue. I look forward to answering any questions you may have.[107]

Author Contact Information

Ronald O'Rourke
Specialist in Naval Affairs
rorourke@crs.loc.gov, 7-7610

---

[107] Testimony [prepared statement] of Deputy Assistant Secretary of Defense Robert Scher, Asian and Pacific Security Affairs, Office of the Secretary of Defense, before the Subcommittee on East Asian and Pacific Affairs, Senate Committee on Foreign Relations, United States Senate, July 15, 2009, [hearing on] Maritime Issues and Sovereignty Disputes in East Asia, 7 pp.